P9-EGD-060

297g

Mr Murphy,

This has been our story! You have always commanded our purpose & our hearts, soul, mind, your heart + what you have headed toward.

thanks for what you have done.

9/1/09

In Our Every Deliberation

Mark & Gini Barker
10 Prospect Street
Boscawen, NH 03303-1216
USA

"In our every deliberation
we must consider the impact of our decisions
on the next seven generations."

From the Great Law of the Haudenosaunee

Published by Seventh Generation
60 Lake Street, Burlington, Vermont 05401
www.seventhgeneration.com

Copyright 2009 by Jeffrey Hollender
All rights reserved. No part of this book may be reproduced, scanned, or distributed in any printed or electronic form without prior permission.

ISBN: 1-4392-3383-7
ISBN-13: 9781439233832

To order additional copies, please contact us.
BookSurge
www.booksurge.com
1-866-308-6235
orders@booksurge.com

In Our Every Deliberation

An Introduction to Seventh Generation

By Jeffery Hollander

Chief Inspired Protagonist

2009

Contents

Introduction

Welcome to Seventh Generation. The choice to join our community is both a commitment to helping us make the world a better place and a commitment to your own growth and development. It's also a commitment to supporting the growth of our company. Yet we believe that we can't grow the business without the growth of everyone in our community. All possibility and potential begins in our own hearts and minds. Our ability to transform the world into a sustainable, just, and equitable place for all its inhabitants starts with our own consciousness of the role we are willing to play. This is a process that is not for the faint of heart.

The journey you are joining is unlike any other you are likely to take in your career because it's one driven by the answer to a question that business has not been designed to answer. "What does the world need most that we are uniquely able to provide?"

This question embraces the vast potential business has to be a positive force for change rather than simply an engine for the use of capital and the creation of wealth. It's a question that forces us to explore how we support the development of the new spirits, fresh minds, and different thinking needed to respond to the huge challenges and boundless opportunity now facing our tiny planet.

The purpose of this book is to help create a brave new group of business leaders (that's you!) committed to ensuring that business realizes its highest potential and to endow them with the capabilities and the will needed to get the job done. This will require that you realize both your own fullest potential and that of the business, a potential that includes financial gain but is not primarily driven by it.

This capability and the will to use it is critical to the world's future, and it is the only way that corporate leaders will be able to see and seize the "whole" opportunity inherent in the possibilities of business, possibilities that if realized will create the shared wealth necessary for a sustainable planet and a world built on peace, justice, and equity.

If that world sounds like an unlikely or even foolishly impossible dream, it's not. Tucked away in corners of the corporate world that are just out of view for most of us, it's already beginning to happen.

From countless experiments in micro-enterprise all over the world, to the members of the Business Alliance for Local Living Economies (BALLE) here in the United States, the revolution is unfolding. In the midst of our current financial and ecological struggles, these efforts are more essential than ever before. Those that remain on the sidelines will most certainly miss the great opportunities they'll create and may even end up as casualties of a competitive landscape that is sure to embrace the coming reality.

That reality needs your help if it is to succeed. In exchange, the journey toward it will provide the most powerful potential for you to enrich your life and fulfill your dreams. No less important, your opportunity as an "owner" of the company will ensure you participate fairly and equitably in the value you create. All you have to do is be willing to open your mind, your heart, and your imagination to possibilities that may at first feel unlikely if not foolhardy.

Welcome to Seventh Generation!

Jeffrey Hollender,
Chief Inspired Protagonist
January 2009

Foreword

I. The Role of Business in Society

Business is the de facto organizing principle of life in the industrialized world, and it is rapidly assuming that role everywhere on the planet. As our central organizing force, it shapes the way we think, what and who we aspire to be, and the framework upon which we live our lives.

While a handful of those running businesses today have some inkling of this power, almost no one understands the true potential that business holds to provide the solution for virtually all the challenges that face our world today. For it will not be governments, NGOs, religious organizations, or individuals that take the lead in the 21st Century. It must and will be business. The question is simply one of purpose: What effect on the world do we seek to have? Are we pursuing our hopes and dreams or merely the simple perpetuation of the dangerous path that we have already, however unconsciously, embarked upon?

Business has become the most powerful influence in our society for a wide variety of interconnected reasons. On the top of my list are the most obvious: the growth and evolution of the multinational corporation, political systems that are freely bought and sold by business interests, a global capitalistic economy that has preempted virtually all other economic structures, and the freedom business enjoys to recklessly acquire, use, sell, and destroy natural resources.

There are other agents reinforcing this dominance. The Internet, for example, provides invaluable support and exponentially enhances the capabilities and efficiency of business. There are tax structures that favor business and its already wealthy leaders. Global free trade agreements that grease the wheels of commerce further still. And the misguided belief that we can *all* benefit and grow rich by marching along in lockstep with the corporate world's private economic interests, a conviction that predominates despite a vast preponderance of evidence that not enough wealth is "trickling down" and that too many boats lie swamped in the rising tide.

Last but certainly not least, as David Putnam articulates so well in "Bowling Alone," there exists a pervasive collective withdrawal, shared covertly or overtly by the majority of us, from the social structures and balancing measures that could provide much needed restraint and even a harmonizing influence on the ever-more pervasive power of business.

The result of these and other forces is a global economic system that works extremely well in highly selective ways but whose sheer dominance over our affairs has created a host of unintended consequences. These include the massive negative effects of all the externalities that business has so efficiently avoided. These negative effects include but are by no means limited to global warming, the extinction of countless species, polluted air and water, toxic chemicals that fill our bodies, the depletion of virtually every natural resource with which we have been blessed, hunger, poverty, inequality, and the sense of hopelessness and disempowerment that describe the way all too many people feel at the end of every work day. These effects live outside the balance sheet of the business world and outside the ways that we measure the health of our global economy.

There are many other kinds of unintended consequences to business' unrestrained supremacy. Corporatism, for example, has convinced us that artifacts are more important than relationships and community. That our cars, flat screen TVs, cell phones, jewelry, and clothing are more important than our values. That what we should prize most is what we can buy, and that what we buy is the thing that defines who and what we are.

Is business to blame for all this? Of course not. Many if not most of us have been willing if unconscious participants in this unfolding drama. We have pursued the path of least resistance and closed our eyes to the effects on our planet and on our own souls that taking this path has had. Yet there is an immense irony in all this, for even as business has become the world's chief organizing principle, this principle has created a world in which neither we nor the businesses we build can survive much longer in their current state.

Correcting this situation and changing the face of business will not be easy because business has, at least to the uninformed eye, generally proven itself to be the most efficient way to get stuff done, whether building bridges, operating communications networks, providing disaster relief, curing disease, or running prisons. Companies run wars. They print currency. They orchestrate elections. Indeed, much of what has traditionally been left in the hands of government is being sold off to the highest bidder or the governments' closest corporate friends. From highways and dams to municipal water and health care systems, business is assuming the roles that government has historically played as the provider of basic services and the manager of infrastructure. And it is likely to continue to do so.

At the same time, business has been particularly adept at creating and reinforcing the current experience of life in the industrialized world. It designs the way we listen to music, experience art, imagine relationships, make friends, decide what to read, how to dress, where to vacation, and what to talk about. In these and other ways, it perpetuates itself by empowering the very ideas that suck us ever deeper into the narrowly focused future from which we must now escape.

Ironically this unrivaled power is the very thing that makes business the force most able to unite us. Unlike those things that tend to divide, like religion, politics, nationalism, and ethnicity, business transcends boundaries in a way no other element of modern life can. Yet there is a certain neutrality at play in this influence, for within a single company there exists every possible worldview, religious belief, ethnicity, and political perspective—all working side by side in synchronicity, pursuing one common goal: making the next quarter's numbers.

So what have we learned as a society when it comes to managing the role of business in society? Very little. In general, business manages us. Despite the faulty notion that business has begun to embrace corporate responsibility, the triple bottom line, sustainability, and other seemingly beneficial new ideas, pitiful little real progress has been made. We have lost the ability to see the forest or the trees. The mechanics of the system within which we live have receded out of view. We see the effects but rarely the causes of what ails so much of the modern world.

Contrary to what you may think after reading all this, I am anything but a pessimist. One cannot do the work that needs to be done unless one is a perpetually irrepressible optimist. Pessimism will only ensure that the tank that holds the energy needed to design the future runs out of fuel midcourse. Optimism, on the other hand, will drive success. Yes, there is an endless flow of sad and angering news that seems these days to connect each moment to the next. But it is possibility that makes life worth living. And given what I see as the necessity for a better future to unfold, there is, at least for me, no other choice.

II. Other Possibilities

As Einstein might have said, everything is relative. There is no one reality. What we see as "real" is determined by our respective vantage points: reality looks very different for a family in my town in Vermont than it does for a family in the heart of Sudan. This subjective understanding of reality is shaped not only by what we see, but what we *don't* see—the information that's left out. Consciously or unconsciously, we all have a personal lens through which we frame the world. And as we know from following the eye of the camera in a movie or TV program, the incomplete picture this lens provides is often misleading. The close-up view of a beautiful flower can pull back to reveal the garbage heap in which it grows. And this truth poses a question: Just how wide a lens are we willing to look through in pursuit of a more complete truth?

Widening the lens, of course, is not an easy thing to do. Society is full of institutions that pressure us to look at life quite narrowly. In fact, almost everything we learn encourages us to restrict the filters through which we allow ourselves to see. Success in today's world is often based on the ability to master a very slim slice of that world. We have become, it is said, a nation of specialists. Biology legend E.O. Wilson, for example, became famous studying a single creature: the ant. At NASA, there are people whose entire careers are built around a single system inside a single spacecraft. Business often leads the way in supporting these kinds of specialization within specialization. And with each ever-narrower sliver into which we slice our individual worlds comes a perspective that is more deeply compartmentalized and disconnected from the whole.

We must widen our lenses to more fully understand the inter-relationships and interdependencies between all things, and better grasp our own responsibilities, opportunities, and impacts. Business must do the same. Understanding complex relationships necessitates open and honest dialogue. It means creating a safe environment in which tough and complex questions can be asked, one in which dissent and self-expression are encouraged, and in which we're willing to hear and act upon harsh criticism.

On my desk sits a pile of corporate responsibility reports. These reports were ostensibly designed to tell us the whole truth about the impact of business and the effect it has on our world. They are full of beautiful, idyllic pictures of sunrises, waterfalls, and fresh mountain streams. They are packed with smiling faces of joyous, contented people of all colors. What an incredible picture of the world this is. And what a limited, dis ingenuous, and dishonest one! It is a much too narrow view that omits the bad news, the efforts that failed, and the shortfalls between where things are and where they ought to be. It is the simplistic picture spun from this sort of incomplete honestly that has reduced corporate responsibility to a series of boxes to be checked. More tragically, it has prevented companies from holding themselves to the higher standards the future demands because we can't own up to the whole truth of the present, which is quite simply this: no company on the planet comes close to modeling behavior that is truly responsible or sustainable and no business has yet managed to show us what the ideal corporate citizen could and should look like.

If I had a room full of the CEOs of the Fortune 500 and asked who among them was running a responsible business, 500 hands would shoot up in the air. How is that possible? Because they all use their own rules and their own definition of corporate responsibility. In fact, when I lecture to MBA students about what it means to be a responsible business, I often say that it's like playing a game with no boundaries, where all the referees use different rules and no one can ever agree about who won the game.

Companies today have all created their own reality in which they believe their own version of "responsibility" to be true. That's obviously dangerous. We need solid boundaries, clear rules and definitions, and a much greater transparency and accountability allowing us to genuinely see who's really winning the game.

III. The Purpose and Possibility of Business

Corporate responsibility and, more recently, corporate sustainability have been billed as the way forward for businesses committed to taking responsibility for all of their stakeholders. And while this is a welcome development it is one that sadly falls well short of what is needed. Something much deeper and more vital is required, something we at Seventh Generation call corporate consciousness, which sees sustainability as an important step on the journey to a regenerative state in which the activities of business actually serve to improve rather than simply maintain our social and environmental support systems.

This never-ending journey toward corporate consciousness plays out in the everyday decisions and struggles we face in running our businesses. For all companies that follow it, it is a path full of mistakes, confusion, and compromise. Sometimes the adventure involves making things worse before they get better. Other times, it's about walking so far down trails we've never traveled that we wind up lost.

But it is also about the wonderful, passionate efforts of millions of people at thousands of businesses accomplishing amazing things. Setbacks and progress are not mutually exclusive; oftentimes they are one and the same. And unless we remember this and celebrate the good, the bad *and* the ugly, we will fail. We'll be so myopically focused on the close-up of the flower that we may never get around to cleaning up the garbage dump that surrounds it.

The purpose of this handbook is to set you on Seventh Generation's path so that you can join us on our journey to redefine the purpose and possibility of business. It is a look at what our business and business in general might and indeed must become in the next 10, 50, or even 100 years. It is about how to lead a conscious business and how to lead a business to consciousness. Even though the trajectory generated yesterday has, for better or worse, defined most of what will happen tomorrow, we can and must create new patterns. And we must understand that they will take time to emerge as we unlearn the past, and become conscious enough of the present to begin to design what we will do in the future.

At its heart, this is a both a guide for how I want to lead the rest of my business life, and for the journey I hope you'll join me on. I hope to also help you more fully understand what you have signed up for and where it all came from. Hopefully it will also inspire others who are thinking about joining us as partners, friends, investors, or advisors. My highest hope is that the words inside will serve as both a practical guide and a source of inspiration that helps us all "be the change we wish to see in the world."

Chapter 1
The Limits and Possibilities of Corporate Responsibility

1.1 What's Driving This New Business Imperative?

Though my deeply cynical point of view may not suggest it, for 20 years I have been at the center of the corporate responsibility movement. As a result of this long tenure, I've become one of its experts, and corporate responsibility itself has become the subject with which I'm most often associated.

In February 2004, I wrote a book entitled *What Matters Most: How a Small Group of Pioneers Is Teaching Social Responsibility to Big Business, and Why Big Business Is Listening.* It was in many respects a critical history of the movement. (In 2010, my next book, *Good Company*, will be published. This new book will look forward and examine how business can make the transition from being "less bad" to "good.")

My work in the field of corporate responsibility has given me a rare perspective on its evolution. And it allows me to safely say that I've seen more change in the past 12 months than in the preceding 19 years.

Today we truly live in a brave new world, and it's led to multinational companies doing things that would have been unimaginable just a few years ago. For example, in 2007 the yogurt company Danone (now the proud owner of Stonyfield Farm) built a factory in a joint venture with the

Grameen Bank in Bangladesh. All the revenue and profits will end up not on Danone's bottom line but will instead be reinvested in the project. The factory cost $500,000, and if the scheme works, ultimately 50 more like it will be built, a total capital investment of $25 million. The project relies on local Grameen microborrowers buying cows to produce the necessary milk, which will be sold to the factory; on Grameen microvendors, who will sell the yogurt door to door; and on Grameen's 6.6 million members, who will purchase the final product for their kids.

According to Fortune magazine:

"Danone estimates that it will provide income for 1,600 people within a 20-mile radius of the plant. Biodegradable cups made from corn-starch, solar panels for electricity generation, and rainwater collection vats make the enterprise environmentally friendly. 'We're saying that profit maximization is not going to be the only way to measure value,' says Emmanuel Faber, Danone's former CFO. What could be the cause of this new passion among the world's largest businesses to make the world a better place? It might have something to do with the fact that leading management consulting firms now consider responsible business essential to corporate strategy."

That's true, and it's a remarkable development for which evidence abounds. A November 2006 McKinsey & Co, internal white paper noted that "the contract between businesses and the society in which they operate is changing quickly. Societal pressure is escalating, and companies are finding themselves increasingly on the defensive. By incorporating society's demands into their strategic planning, however, companies can turn apparently threatening sociopolitical trends to their advantage. Companies that successfully bring society into strategy will create enormous value, as well as contribute to the greater good. They will have better growth potential."

Indeed, according to Harvard Business School Professor Lynn Sharp Paine's groundbreaking 2002 book *Value Shift: Why Companies Must Merge Social and Financial Imperatives to Achieve Superior Results*, responsible businesses actually perform better financially that those that are less committed to corporate citizenship. While critics of the book greeted its publication by questioning the methodology of the many studies Paine referenced, time has proven her to be not just correct but visionary. For in the years that followed, the reinforcing data just kept pouring in.

My favorite of all these studies was one of the simplest. On October 27, 2005 the Financial Times reported that if you had bought stock in all the public companies listed in Milton Moskowitz's ranking of the 100 best companies to work for in 1998, when it was first published by Fortune magazine, and held that stock until 2005, you would have made twice the annualized return of the S&P 500 Index. If you had sold each year and reinvested in the new list, you would have made three times the S&P return.

That's a finding echoed by a 2007 report from investment banking standard bearer Goldman Sachs, which revealed that those companies that are considered social and environmental leaders are also delivering the best stock market performance, with returns that top their less responsible peers by an average of 25%.

Profit motives aside, business has also embraced corporate responsibility as a result of the transparency that has been forced on corporate America by the Internet; increasing pressure from NGOs and activists groups; the influence of pension funds and socially responsible investors; the imperative to protect brands, reputation, and other intangible assets that now account for almost 75% of the value of the average business; and the impact it has on attracting and retaining talent.

1.2 Reporting and Its Limitations

In 1989, when we raised the money to launch Seventh Generation, we described ourselves as a socially responsible business. It was a self-portrait that many considered quirky and most thought was downright strange. Still others described us in ways that were far less kind. Social responsibility and business were not words that belonged together in the same sentence, let alone one that was attached to a business plan whose purpose was to raise start-up capital.

We were sailing through an uncharted sea, buffeted by winds of indifference and waves of callous disregard. But we were not alone. There was a tiny band of other companies that had attached themselves to this same idea. Ben & Jerry's, the Body Shop, and Patagonia were the best known of the bunch, and none of them could ever imagine having anything in common with Wal-Mart, British Petroleum, or McDonalds.

We believed it was becoming clear that Milton Freedman's thesis, that the exclusive responsibility of business is to maximize returns to shareholders, was going to be an increasingly dangerous idea as the 20th century closed and a new millennium began. But we were largely outcasts from the corporate world.

Lynn S. Paine's *Value Shift* correctly argues that companies can't consider themselves amoral or apart from society anymore and the relationship between companies and society at large necessitates bringing a moral dimension to decision making. This was the higher ideal we and our kindred companies embraced with enthusiasm. We could be better, and we would do better, and if not at least we were going to die trying.

Cut to 2004, and corporate responsibility is an idea now often being discussed, though usually not understood, in virtually every corporate board room in America. Research from the Center for Corporate Citizenship at Boston College and the US Chamber of Commerce notes that 83% of surveyed companies said good corporate citizenship helps the bottom line, and 59% felt these practices improve company image and reputation.

Suddenly there were corporate responsibility conferences, consulting companies, magazines, web sites, and newsletters. And you were more likely to hear the CEO of Starbucks, Nike, or Hewlett Packard espousing the virtues of responsible business than Ben Cohen or Anita Roddick, who by then had moved on to other endeavors.

The common thread running through this movement was corporate responsibility reporting. It became the primary way that companies publicly declared their commitment to "responsibility" and made their case that they voluntarily held themselves to a different standard, were willing to be judged accordingly, and were, in fact, worthy of the label.

Seventh Generation completed its first Corporate Responsibility report in 2002. It was an arduous task. In 2004, we upgraded our report by following the Global Reporting Initiative guidelines, which were developed for large, primarily public companies. The process was complex, expensive, and, to be perfectly blunt, an enormous pain in the ass. But the GRI guidelines represent the gold standard in reporting, and we figured that we needed to support this standard and show our leadership by using it.

In each subsequent year, we continued to publish an annual report. While we won several awards for excellence in reporting, I'm not sure that the reports were read by very many. And while each report was better than the last, our own efforts at what we now call Corporate Consciousness left much to be desired.

Our 2007 report, *Spheres Of Influence*, was emblematic of the situation in which we found ourselves. It was our best report yet. But it opened with a letter from me that discussed a large and painful failure we had experienced on the transparency front. For all the good we were able to report on, we were in essence just as "less bad" as everyone else.

While some 1,200 companies around the world issued CSR reports in 2007 and 2008, less than 260 used the GRI guidelines, and in the US only 28 companies issued GRI-based reports. Unfortunately, most non-GRI reports are incomplete at best and deceiving at worst. Think of reports that don't follow GRI guidelines as you would financial statements that don't follow standard accounting rules. They're so free to twist the data around to suit their purposes that they're all but meaningless where it counts.

If reporting is critical to allowing stakeholder assessment of business responsibility progress and a good process has been developed that most companies won't use, where does that leave us? What does that say about business' commitment to responsibility and to the transparency needed to gauge it?

Some countries, including South Africa and several in the European Union nations, have already passed or are considering passing legislation that would require more complete disclosures. Nothing of the kind is even on the horizon in the US though consideration of such a rule is not nearly the hopeless dream it once was now that the Obama administration has taken the reins in Washington.

David Vogel, in his 2004 book, *The Market for Virtue: The Potential and Limits of Corporate Social Responsibility*, describes the challenge that business faces, a challenge that has changed less since 2004 than it would appear:
"Is CSR having or likely to have a significant impact on the behavior of firms?" he asks. "Is it succeeding, or is it likely to succeed, in having firms play a more 'coherent' role in addressing the really big social and environmental challenges of both today's and tomorrow's

world?[1] To what extent and on what dimensions are firms becoming more responsible 'corporate citizens?' Is corporate performance increasingly being measured and evaluated by a 'triple bottom line,' one which judges the impact of business on 'economic prosperity, environmental quality, and social justice' and not only shareholder value?[2] Is 'civic regulation' a viable alternative to government regulation? Most fundamentally, are business norms and what managers consider efficient and appropriate behavior changing?[3] In short, are corporations becoming more virtuous?

"Much writing on CSR is highly polarized, with its proponents often heralding the long-term impact of the myriad pressures on and incentives for business to improve its social performance, while its critics are either skeptical that significant changes have occurred or are likely to take place, or believe that corporations have changed, but that these changes are undermining the business system.[4]

"This book takes a more nuanced position. Its central argument is that while the CSR movement has measurably improved the performance of some firms in some areas, its overall impact has been and will remain more modest than many of its advocates claim, or hope— or some of their critics fear. There is a business case for CSR, but there are also important business constraints on CSR. Much writing on CSR focuses on the former, but neglects to appreciate the significance of the latter. Many of the claims for the impact of CSR on improving business practices mistakenly assume that because some companies are behaving more responsibly in some areas, additional firms can be expected to behave more responsibly across multiple areas. This assumption is misinformed.

"CSR is not just about more sophisticated corporate public relations or 'greenwashing.' There have in fact been some substantive changes in corporate behavior and a number of these have improved social welfare. There is a market for virtue, but the ability of the market to supply virtue is also limited. The market for virtue does have positive externalities: issues raised by public debates about CSR help inform public awareness and political debate about corporate practices. But because of the limited ability of the market for virtue to internalize externalities, pervasive market failures remain.
"CSR reflects both the strengths and shortcomings of market capitalism. On one hand, it promotes social and environmental innovation by business, encouraging or prompting firms to adopt new policies, strategies, and products, some of which may also be profitable. It

also provides a way for consumers, investors, and employees to 'vote' their social preferences via the market and thus influence corporate policies.[5] Most importantly, it provides a way for citizens to use their roles as consumers and investors to increase the public visibility of a wide range of business decisions, thus subjecting them to increased public scrutiny.

"But on the other hand, precisely because CSR is voluntary or market-driven, companies will only engage in CSR to the extent that it makes business sense for them to do so. But to the extent that CSR is costly—and companies cannot recover those costs through higher prices, additional sales, a better reputation, lower wages, more committed employees, or lower costs—they are unlikely to behave more responsibly. If CSR expenditures depress earnings, then the only way companies will behave more responsibly is if government regulations require them to do so. Under these circumstances, private regulation is a second best solution. While CSR can under some circumstances complement or supplement the role of government, private authority is typically not a viable or effective substitute for public authority. This limits the overall ability of CSR to improve corporate social and environmental performance."

Chapter 2
What Is Sustainability?

"We cannot have well humans on a sick planet. We cannot have a viable human economy by devastating the Earth's economy. We cannot survive if the conditions of life itself are not protected. Not only our physical being, but our souls, our minds, imagination, and emotions depend on our immediate experience of the natural world. There is in the industrial process no poetry, no elevation or fulfillment of mind or emotions comparable to that experienced in the magnificence of the sea, the mountains, the sky, the stars at night, the flowers blooming in the meadows, the flights and song of the birds. As the natural world diminishes in its splendor, so human life diminishes in its fulfillment of both the physical and the spiritual aspects of our being. Not only is it the case with humans, but with every mode of being. The wellbeing of each member of the Earth community is dependent on the wellbeing of the Earth itself."

Thomas Berry

"With great respect to those who assert the so-called 'primacy' of key social and economic goals (such as the elimination of poverty or the attainment of universal human rights), it must be said loud and clear that these are *secondary* goals: all else is conditional upon learning to live sustainably within the Earth's systems and limits. Not only is the pursuit of biophysical sustainability non-negotiable; it's preconditional.

"Having said that, these are really two sides of the same coin. On the one hand, social sustainability is entirely dependent upon ecological sustainability. As we continue to undermine nature's capacity to provide humans with essential services (such as clean water, a stable climate, and so on) and resources (such as food and raw materials), both individuals and nation states will be subjected to growing amounts of pressure. Conflict will grow, and threats to public health and personal safety will increase in the face of ecological degradation."

Jonathan Porritt, *Capitalism as if the World Matters*

On August 9, 2007, a Google search on the word "sustainability" produced 40,600,000 results. On August 10th, there were 40,700,000 results, an increase of 100,000 entries in just 24 hours. By August 14th, the listings had climbed to over 41 million. From a listing for Donella Meadows, founder of the Sustainability Institute and lead author of *Limits to Growth,* to the Dow Jones Sustainability Indexes, the United Parcel Service Corporate Sustainability Report, sustainable diapers, and even the Sustainability Store, sustainability is a hot idea. Never mind that few really understand it, let alone use the word appropriately, sustainability has become what businesses, governments, hospitals, and schools want to do, what the media wants to write about, and consumers want to achieve.

There are almost as many definitions of sustainability as there are people who are inclined to try and define it. The Forum for the Future defines sustainability as "A dynamic process which enables all people to realize their potential and to improve their quality of life in ways that simultaneously protect and enhance the Earth's life support systems." One of the most often-cited definitions of sustainability is the one created by the Brundtland Commission, led by the former Norwegian Prime Minister Gro Harlem Brundtland, which defined sustainable development as development that "meets the needs of the present without compromising the ability of future generations to meet their own needs." For its part, Wikipedia defines sustainability as "the capacity to maintain a certain process or state indefinitely." Clearly sustainability relates to the continuity of economic, social, and institutional aspects of human society, as well as the non-human environment. It embodies the intent to provide the best outcomes for both human and natural ecosystems now and into the indefinite future.

David Bohm, a physicist and author of *The Implicate Order*, a book I aspire to finish reading some day, could be considered the grandfather of today's sustainability movement. Bohm provides the philosophical underpinnings of modern systems thinking upon which the concept of sustainability rests. He writes about the essential interrelatedness and interdependence of all phenomena—physiological, social, and cultural. Nothing can be understood in isolation; everything has to be seen as part of a unified whole. It is only through abstraction that things look separate. We are each "the whole of mankind. That's the idea of the implicate order—that everything is enfolded in everything else. The entire past is enfolded in us in a very subtle way. If you reach deeply into yourself, you are reaching into the very essence of mankind...We are all connected. If this could be taught, and if people could understand it, we would have a very different conscious-ness.... People create barriers between each other by their fragmentary thought. Each one operates separately. When these barriers have been dis-solved, then there arises one mind." (from Synchronicity, pp. 80-81)

Our inability to design a world that functions in a sustainable man-ner begins with our own mind. We have been taught to think in a compart-mentalized way that deconstructs the world. We no longer see its interre-latedness and have forgotten that everything is ultimately connected. Thus we mistakenly believe we can act in ways that do not affect everyone and everything else. Systems thinking, the foundation for designing a sustain-able business, begins with learning to think differently.

This deeper concept of sustainability has been developed over time by many individuals such as Janine Benyus, author of the book *Biomimicry: Innovation Inspired by Nature*; Amory Lovins, author and co-founder of the Rocky Mountain Institute; and Paul Hawken, an environmentalist, entre-preneur, and author.

Natural Capitalism by Hawken and Lovins provided one of the first systemic guides to reconciling ecological and economic goals. Hawken is the founder of the Natural Capital Institute, a small research group fo-cused on better understanding principles and practices leading to social justice and environmental restoration. He was an early and aggressive pro-ponent of more definitive corporate responsibility standards that would help people select and support businesses "that will conform (not only) to (their) hopes and aspirations, but also their desire to allocate their sav-ings and investments in a manner that will promote social and ecological change...it hardly matters how a company operates its business if where it is going is harmful."

Janine Benyus, one of the sustainability field's most brilliant minds, developed the concept of biomimicry, the rather simple idea that if we can understand the way in which nature works to acquire and store energy, build bridges and tunnels, create community, and manage populations, we might find some clues as to what we need to do to create a more sustainable business.

Janine Benyus describes biomimicry as "coming from bios, meaning life, and mimesis, meaning to imitate." It's a design discipline that studies nature's best ideas and then imitates these architectures and processes to solve human problems. Studying a leaf to invent a better solar cell is an example of this "innovation inspired by nature." Benyus has worked at the fringes of business but has yet to breakthrough to the mainstream despite the fact that there are few other people more deserving of being discovered than she. She writes:

> "The core idea, is that nature, imaginative by necessity, has already solved many of the problems we are grappling with. Animals, plants, and microbes are the consummate engineers. They have found what works, what is appropriate, and most important, what lasts here on Earth. This is the real news of biomimicry: After 3.8 billion years of research and development, failures are fossils, and what surrounds us is the secret to survival.

> "Like the viceroy butterfly imitating the monarch, we humans are imitating the best and brightest organisms in our habitat. We are learning, for instance, how to grow food like a prairie, build ceramics like an abalone, create color like a peacock, self-medicate like a chimp, compute like a cell, and run a business like a hickory forest.

> "The conscious emulation of life's genius is a survival strategy for the human race, a path to a sustainable future. The more our world looks and functions like the natural world, the more likely we are to endure on this home that is ours, but not ours alone."

Applying sustainability to business as a primary focus and using his own business as a real world laboratory, Ray Anderson of carpet manufacturer Interface is the elder statesman of the movement and one of the pioneers in the field. Anderson believes that, "understanding and adopting sustainable business practices requires a new awareness of the world; the whole world, its natural systems and all of its species. It requires a deeper understanding of how the Earth works, and how man's processes affect nature's delicate balance.

"Understanding sustainability requires an awareness of how everything we do, everything we take, everything we make, and everything we waste affects nature's balance, and how our actions will ultimately affect our children and the children of all species."

The recent history of sustainability focuses on two interrelated streams of thought. In 1970s and 80s, when the concept of sustainability was little known and rarely discussed, it polarized people whenever it popped up because it stood for what we should not do: buy so much stuff, build such big houses, use so many non-renewable resources, travel so far to go to work, create so much garbage. Donella Meadows, lead author of *Limits to Growth* was one of the first to widely promote this point of view. More recently when Al Gore told us that global warming was the greatest threat to human civilization (not to mention multi-million dollar beach houses from Malibu to the Hamptons!), we all decided we wanted to be sustainable, though most of us forgot about the buy-less-stuff part.

The question of the extent to which sustainability will actually require changes to the lifestyles of those in both the developed and the developing world is still being debated. Fortune 500 companies will uniformly tell you that we can get there through greater energy and resource efficiency, left leaning environmental thinkers like Bill McKibben will argue that we have created a vision of happiness that is so dependent on the vast accumulation of material wealth that nothing short of a new vision of the American Dream will do the trick. He writes:

> "Alan Durning found that in 1991 the average American family owned twice as many cars, drove two and a half times as far, used twenty-one times as much plastic, and traveled twenty five times farther by air than did the average family in 1951...Our homes are bigger: the size of new homes has doubled since 1970." (*Deep Economy*, p. 34)

> "Since the mid 1960s, Alexander Astin and his colleagues have been asking over 200,000 first-year college students in the United States what is important to them in life. The percentage of students who believe that it is very important or essential to 'develop a meaningful philosophy of life' decreased from over 80 percent in the late 1960's to around 40 percent in the late 1990's. At the same time, the percentage that believes that it is very important or essential to be 'very well off financially' has risen from just over 40 percent to over 70 percent. Society's value-making machine is an effective one." (Jonathon Porritt, *Capitalism as if the World Matters*, p. 311)

While we know this vast accumulation has imposed a huge impact on the planet, what else has this desperate process of accumulation created? Are we happier? Do we feel better because we have more stuff?

"Looking at survey figures from around the world, there remains a strong correlation between subjective perceptions of wellbeing and per capita income. But research by Robert Lane, Ed Diener, and Ruut Veenhoven clearly demonstrates that, beyond a certain point, the correlation first weakens and then disappears. People may set that threshold at different levels; but it is clear that the law of diminishing returns applies as much here is as in any other area. In *The Loss of Happiness in Market Democracies*, Robert Lane (2000) describes this as 'the waning power of income to yield that ephemeral good utility,' and castigates both academics and politicians for being in thrall to the 'economistic fallacy' that, beyond poverty or basic subsistence levels, higher incomes will automatically increase levels of subjective wellbeing." (*Capitalism as if the World Matters*, p. 53)

In fact not only is there a dubious relationship between happiness and the accumulation of wealth, it's hard to find evidence of a causal relationship. This seems somewhat more true in Europe that in the US.

"There is a growing body of evidence which shows that things are actually getting worse in terms of real mental wellbeing. There is a growing consensus among psychiatric researchers that rates of depression, for instance, have been on the increase since the 1950's, especially among the young. In November 2002, a report from the Joseph Rowntree Foundation compared 10,000 people born in 1958 with 10,000 born in 1970. While in their mid 20's, both groups were questioned about their mental health. Among the post-World War II generation, just 7 percent of those questioned had a tendency to non-clinical depression; among those born in 1970, the figure had doubled to 14 percent. (*Capitalism as if the World Matters*, p. 54)

"In 2002, the Institute of Optimum Nutrition surveyed around 22,000 UK citizens, most living in towns and cities, and most below the age of 30. They found that:

- 76 percent of people are regularly tired;
- 58 percent suffer from mood swings;
- 52 percent feel apathetic and unmotivated;
- 50 percent suffer from anxiety;
- 47 percent have difficulty sleeping;
- 43 percent have poor memories or struggle to concentrate; and
- 42 percent suffer from depression."

(Capitalism as if the World Matters, p. 55)

So if we haven't secured our health and wellbeing, what have we accomplished?

- Since 1997, wild fish harvests have fallen 13 percent.

- Pesticide use has risen dramatically worldwide, from 0.49 kilograms per hectare in 1961 to 2 kilograms per hectare in 2004.

- Economic damages from weather-related disasters hit an unprecedented $204 billion in 2005, nearly doubling the previous record of $112 billion set in 1998.

- Global advertising spending increased 2.4 percent to a record $570 billion in 2005. Nearly half of this spending was in the United States.

- Air travel hit new records as well: in 2004, 1.9 billion passengers traveled 3.4 trillion kilometers. Yet only 5 percent of the world's population has ever flown.

- Over half of the world's 7,000 languages are endangered.

- One billion individuals, or one in every three urbanites, live in "slums," areas where people cannot secure one or more of life's basic necessities: clean water, sanitation, sufficient living space, durable housing, or secure tenure.

- As of late 2005, an estimated 20 percent of the world's coral reefs had been "effectively destroyed," while 50 percent are threatened in the short or long term.

- Half the world's tropical and temperate forests are now gone. The rate of deforestation in the tropics continues at about an acre a second. About half the wetlands and a third of the mangroves are gone.

- An estimated 90 percent of the large predator fish are gone, and 75 percent of marine fisheries are now overfished or fished to capacity. Species are disappearing at rates about a thousand times faster than normal. The planet has not seen such a spasm of extinction in since the dinosaurs disappeared sixty-five million years ago.

- Persistent toxic chemicals can now be found by the dozens in essentially each and every one of us.

(All figures from *Vital Signs 2006-2007*, Worldwatch Institute, July 2006, additional statistics from *The Bridge at the Edge of the World* by Gustave Speth)

What has generally escaped focus, attention, and serious thought is the fact that the idea of sustainability in not exclusively or even primarily about the environment, but rather, as we have discussed is:

"...a dynamic process which enables all people to realize their potential and to improve their quality of life in ways which simultaneously protect and enhance the Earth's life-support systems'—(a definition which) both affirms sustainable development as a dynamic process and emphasizes the importance of social justice and equity in that it has to be made to work for *all* people." (*Capitalism as if the World Matters*, p. 22)

Viewed from this perspective, the challenge we face is even greater. While it is important for business to increase the use of renewable and recycled materials, improve the efficiency of transportation, and reduce the use of toxic chemicals, how many companies are committed to developing "a dynamic process which enables all people to realize their potential?" And we're not just talking about employees, but all of humanity. Though it's not even on the radar of 99% of all businesses, I believe that this aspect of universal human fulfillment is implicit whenever we talk about sustainability

So where do we at Seventh Generation stand? Again, we're less bad than most, but certainly not good or sustainable. As we'll discuss later, our mission, or, as it's called at Seventh Generation, our global imperatives, includes sustainability as a critical focus:

We are committed to approaching everything we do from a systems perspective which allows us to see a world that is endlessly interconnected, in which everything we do affects everything else.

We must ensure that globally, natural resources are used and renewed at a rate that is always below their rate of depletion.

To creating a business where all our products are not just sustainable but restorative, and enhance the potential of all of life's systems.

This commitment is something we call "a promise beyond our ableness," more commonly known as a big, hairy, audacious goal. It's one we are deeply committed to, but one that remains more of a dream than a reality.

How is it that Seventh Generation, a company known as a leader in sustainability, could rate so poorly on scales that measure it? Because we hold ourselves to a much higher standard based upon the true meaning of the word.

Sustainability is the job of everyone at the company, from accounting to marketing, logistics to product development. It will be your job to ensure that we fulfill our commitment it. And for that we will need every last iota of your passion and your imagination.

Chapter 3
Business & Sustainability

3.1 Oil & Water or Peanut Butter & Chocolate?

"If we are to 'rededicate our society to the pursuit of happiness' rather than the goals of growth, efficiency and competitiveness, then we will need to be monitoring people's wellbeing and happiness just as closely as we measure income and gross domestic product (GDP). We should be focusing far more on the problems of mental health; we should be actively investing in activities that promote community life and build social capital; we should eliminate high unemployment altogether; we should rethink our education system—'we should teach the systematic practice of empathy and the desire to serve others'— and be less coy about the importance of moral education; we should get real about family-friendly practices at work; and we should ban all advertising to children!"

(Capitalism as if the World Matters)

"For the most part, capitalism itself has answered the demands that inspired 19th century socialism.... But attainment of these goals has only brought deeper sources of social unease—manipulation by marketers, obsessive materialism, environmental degradation, endemic alienation, and loneliness. In short...in the marketing society, we seek fulfillment but settle for abundance. Prisoners of plenty, we have the freedom to consume instead of the freedom to find our place in the world."

(Clive Hamilton, *Growth Fetish*)

Is the idea of sustainability compatible with capitalism? If so, what fundamental changes must occur within both business and society for sustainability to become a real possibility? Can businesses succeed or even simply survive without imbedding sustainability into their corporate strategies? What are the best examples of companies that have actually begun to transform themselves?

These questions are an appropriate topic for an entire book, if not a series of books. To begin our search for answers, this chapter is framed by the work of Jonathan Porritt in his book on the subject *Capitalism as if the World Matters.* Porritt is Chairman of the UK Sustainable Development Commission, former Chairman of the Ecology Party (now the Green Party), former Director of the Friends of the Earth UK, and current Director of the Forum for the Future, which aims to persuade individual businesses to improve their environmental performance.

The discussion that follows is both dense and complex, something that's not inappropriate for such a challenging topic. It's important to remember as you read it that this is but an introduction to the questions posed above. I would encourage you to read the books referenced below if the subject intrigues you.

3.2 Is the Idea of Sustainability Compatible With Capitalism?

The answer to this question is an unequivocal yes. We do not have the time, the inspiration, or the will to create an alternative to capitalism. All attempts to come up with a new system of commerce have failed to reach meaningful scale or last for any significant duration. The only possibility left to us is to make design changes to both capitalism and business in order to increase our ability to create a sustainable future.

Sustainability, which is often described in the context of sustainable development is rarely looked at in a manner that accepts the central and essential role of business. Porritt frames the question:

> "At its heart, therefore, sustainable development comes right down to one all important challenge: is it possible to conceptualize and then operationalize an alternative model of capitalism—one that allows for the sustainable management of the different capital assets upon which we rely so that the yield from those different assets sustains us now, as well as in the future?
>
> "The case for sustainable development must be reframed if that is to happen. It must be as much about new opportunities for responsible

wealth creation as about outlawing irresponsible wealth creation; it must draw upon a core of ideas and values that speaks directly to people's desire for a higher quality of life, emphasizing enlightened self-interest and personal wellbeing of a different kind." (*Capitalism as if the World Matters*, p. 19-20)

In 1990, Herman Daly put forward four core principles to guide this sustainable development journey:

1. Limit the human scale (or economic throughput) to that which is within the Earth's current capacity.
2. Ensure that technological progress is efficiency-increasing rather than throughput-increasing.
3. For renewable resources, harvesting rates should not exceed regeneration rates (sustained yield); waste emissions should not exceed the assimilative capacities of the receiving environment.
4. Non-renewable resources should be exploited no faster than the rate of creation of renewable substitutes.

Porritt continues:

"We are facing a sustainability crisis because we're consuming our stocks of natural, human and social capital faster than they are being produced. Unless we control the rate of this consumption, we can't sustain these vital stocks in the long-term.

"We believe that by maintaining and trying to increase stocks of these capital assets, we can live off the income without reducing the capital itself. But for this to happen, it is the responsibility of every organization, business or otherwise, to manage these capital assets sustainably.

"There are five types of sustainable capital from where we derive the goods and services we need to improve the quality of our lives.

"*Natural Capital* (also referred to as...) environmental or ecological capital) is any stock or flow of energy and material that yields valuable goods and services. It falls into several categories: resources, some of which are renewable (timber, grain, fish, and water), while others are not (fossil fuels); sinks which absorb, neutralize, or recycle waste; and processes, such as climate regulation. Natural capital is the basis not only of production but of life itself!

"*Human capital* consists of people's health, knowledge, skills, and motivation. All these things are needed for productive work as well as an individual's emotional and spiritual capacities. Enhancing human capital through investment in education and training is central to a flourishing economy.

"*Social capital* takes the form of structures, institutions, networks, and relationships which enable individuals to maintain and develop their human capital in partnership with others, and to be more productive when working together than in isolation. It includes families, communities, businesses, trade unions, voluntary organizations, legal/political systems, and educational and health bodies.

"*Manufactured capital* comprises material goods or fixed assets—tools, machines, buildings and other forms of infrastructure—which contribute to the production process rather than being the output.

"*Financial capital* plays an important role in our economy, enabling the other types of Capital to be owned and traded. But unlike the other types, it has no intrinsic value; whether in shares, bonds, or banknotes, its value is purely representative of natural, human, social, or manufactured capital.

"Sustainable development is the best way to manage these capital assets in the long-term. It is a dynamic process through which organizations can begin to achieve a balance between their environmental, social, and economic activities." (Source: Forum for the Future)

But from a practical perspective, what would this entail? Porritt provides a glimpse:

"Given global population growth and current aspirations for increased material prosperity, Paul Ekins and others have calculated that to achieve environmental sustainability in an affluent industrial country would require a reduction in the environmental intensity of consumption (the environmental impact per unit of consumption) by a factor of about ten (that is, a 90 percent reduction) by about 2050. Thereafter, if economic growth continues, the environmental intensity of consumption will have to continue to decrease, at least at the rate of economic growth for those impacts that are at the threshold of sustainability." (p. 227)

Some would find this an impossible goal. But in fact all we are lacking is vision and leadership. Much of the technology is already in place. What we need is a "Marshall Plan" for sustainability.

James Gustave Speth, in his wonderful book, *The Bridge at the Edge of the World; Capitalism, the Environment, and Crossing From Crisis to Sustainability*, approaches the changes that are required from a different perspective.

> "We must change the very nature of corporations so they become legally accountable to society at large, not just to themselves and their shareholders.

> "We must challenge the current obsession with GDP growth and focus on growth in the areas that truly enhance human well-being: growth in good jobs, in the availability of health care, in education, in the deployment of green technologies, in the incomes of the poor, in security against illness and disability, in infrastructure, and more.

> "We must challenge materialism and consumerism as the source of happiness and seek new values about quality of life, social solidarity, and connectedness to nature.

> "We must transform the market through government action so that it works for the environment, rather than against it.

> "We must transform democracy through deep political reforms that reassert popular control, encouraging locally strong, deliberative democracy and limiting corporate influence.

> "We must forge a new environmental politics that recognizes links among environmentalism, social liberalism, human and civil rights, the fight against poverty, and other issues."

3.3 Working for Change From the Inside Out

Several years ago, I met Phil Angelides, who at the time was the treasurer of CALPERS, the California State Teachers Retirement System, at a small conference on socially responsible investing in Stowe, Vermont, just up the road from where I live. At the time, CALPERS had assets of over $150 billion, and it's sister pension fund had another $100 billion in assets.

Together with $250 billion under management, they were one of the world's most influential investors.

Phil told a story that I'll never forget about why he wouldn't invest in certain pharmaceutical companies. He said, "Oh, I can make plenty of money investing in them, but there's one problem: I figured out that for every $10 I made for my pensioners, they ended up paying $20 in higher drug prices. That was a pretty bad deal."

I was stunned. It was the first time I'd ever heard someone whose job it was to invest money express an understanding of systemic thinking. I shouldn't have been surprised. CALPERS has a long history as an activist investor. Following the tradition started by investors who pressured companies doing business in South Africa to take a stand against apartheid, CALPERS has led other pension firms to push corporate boards on a variety of corporate governance issues from board independence to executive pay.

Mark Gunther, who was for many years Fortune magazine's pioneering reporter on corporate responsibility and is the husband of a grade school friend, wrote in 2003:

> "The social agenda at Calpers and Calstrs is driven by this holistic view of their holdings. Angelides argues that social good generates economic returns for his funds because a healthier society means healthier companies. Calpers's inner-city investments, for instance, might generate not only direct returns (and they do, says Angelides) but also indirect benefits because they curb inequality, reduce the costs of poverty, and create new customers for other companies owned by the fund. Angelides calls this a 'double bottom line'—financial returns and social good. If Calpers, through either its investments or shareholder activism, can support companies that contribute to the health of the economy say by educating their workforce or preventing pollution and penalize those that are antisocial, the fund will ultimately benefit. 'I don't think many companies can be successful in an unsuccessful economy,' Angelides says. Nor can companies thrive, he says, in an economy plagued by environmental woes, health-care costs, or 'great divisions between rich and poor that erupt into social tension.'

"This is an unorthodox approach to pension-fund investment to say the least. Think about what it means for an issue like global warming. Calpers and Calstrs arguably have good reason to pressure automakers and utility companies to reduce their emissions of greenhouse gases because of the threat that global warming poses to the tourism and agriculture companies that are also part of their portfolios."

CALPERS wasn't exactly saying that businesses won't succeed or survive without imbedding sustainability into strategy, but it was getting pretty close. And it was only four years later that consulting firms like McKinsey drew even closer to that notion when, as we saw in Chapter 1, they wrote a white paper introducing the idea that "companies that successfully bring society into strategy will create enormous value, as well as contribute to the greater good. They will have better growth potential, be less vulnerable to product litigation costs, and be better situated to develop win-win solutions with regulators. They will enhance their reputation and position themselves as the shapers and commercial leaders of tomorrow's most attractive markets."

Phil Angelides and CALPERS weren't alone or even the pioneers of this point of view. In some respects Robert Augustus Gardner Monks, could be considered the grandfather of this movement. In 2002, Mark Gunther profiled Monks in Fortune:

"Robert Monks, the scion of a long-established, well-to-do New England family, made up his mind long ago that something was wrong with the way corporations were run in America, and that his mission was to fix it.

"He was an unlikely rebel. Monks graduated from Harvard, where he rowed for the varsity crew, and Harvard Law School. His wife of 49 years, Millie, is a descendant of the Carnegies. He inherited money, became a partner in a Boston law firm, and made a second fortune running a coal-and-oil company.

"His transformation into a corporate reformer began in 1972, while he was campaigning unsuccessfully as a Republican for a U.S. Senate seat in Maine. The story goes that, stopping beside the Penobscot River, Monks noticed big, slick white bubbles of industrial foam, damaging vegetation along its bank. He wondered why the owners or executives of the Great Northern Paper Co., whom he knew, would let that happen. Several years later, after becoming chairman of the Boston Safe Deposit & Trust Co., Monks decided that he was part of the problem. As trustee for $7 billion in assets managed by the bank, he was glancing through proxy statements and preparing to do what he had always done—vote automatically with management—when he came to a proxy from Great Northern.

" 'My God,' he recalls, 'it was the same company that was floating the foam. So, as the English say, the penny dropped. I understood that myself and maybe 50, 60 people like me owned enough of an interest that we could actually have an impact. I began thinking of ownership in very human terms.'

"There are two things you should know about Bob Monks at this point in his story. First, he's a clergyman's son. 'People like me who were taken to church eight times a day during their adolescence remember things like 'Unto whom much is given, much will be required," he says. Second, he is unusually purposeful about his life. When he sold the coal-and-oil company in 1970, he and a partner hired Peter Drucker, for $1,000 a day, to talk with them about what they might do next. Ten years later, after losing a second Senate bid, Monks spent most of a summer at his oceanfront home in Cape Elizabeth, ME, researching the role of corporations in a democracy. He learned, among other things, that pension funds had become the largest owners of U.S. companies, thereby beginning to reaggregate the fragmented base of shareholders. Hoping to transform them into the responsible owners he thought the system lacked, he wrote a mission statement of more than 100 pages that has guided him ever since. 'One of the great virtues of my life,' he says, 'is that I had this epiphany, as it were, when I was about 50, and rich, and I belonged to whatever clubs I ever wanted to join.'

"By then the groundwork for shareholder activism had been laid. Corporate gadflies like the Gilbert brothers, Lewis and John, had persuaded the SEC to enact the first rules governing shareholder proposals in 1942. Later, social reformers like Ralph Nader and Saul Alinsky, along with church groups and foundations, had used shareholder resolutions to pressure companies on social issues like the Vietnam war and apartheid in South Africa. Still to come were the corporate raiders of the 1980s, a more mercenary brand of owners, who took stakes in poorly run companies, threatened takeovers, and drove up their stock prices. They often got rich by taking 'greenmail,' or payments to get them to go away."

In the early 1990s. the business community's betrayal of society was revealed in a stunning series of scandals. From Enron and Tyco to World Com and Imclone, numerous companies showed the world all too clearly that despite the efforts of early corporate responsibility pioneers, much of the trust we had placed in business had been largely misplaced and ill deserved. But there was a silver lining in this dark cloud: In the wake of those sad events, as public trust in business plummeted to deeper and deeper depths, the nascent corporate responsibility movement received a huge boost of attention and recognition that might have otherwise been impossible to attain.

Yet after a decade of growing interest and participation in the practice of corporate responsibility, the business world has made little progress toward true and lasting sustainability. While many companies have improved governance and a handful publish GRI-based corporate responsibility reports, none have successfully balanced the dual challenges of social and environmental responsibility to become genuinely responsible let alone meaningfully sustainable.

Like the business scandals of the early 1990s, the financial crisis of 2008-2009, unparalleled in its global scope and stunning in its level of greed-driven fraud and irresponsible excess, delivered some well-timed further impetus for both the business world and society at large to conduct some much-needed self-examination. It brought into focus issues that I never believed would be so starkly challenged. Amidst the furor that followed, people began to realize that previously unthinkable economic heresies had been right all along:

- Market economics do not produce a healthy economy.

- The current laissez faire regulatory environment has allowed widespread corruption to become institutionalized.

- The measurements that we depend upon to determine the health of our economy ("gross domestic product") are so deeply flawed that they provide meaningless information.

- Our obsession with consumerism is not sustainable and does not produce happiness or wellbeing.

- During the 60s we were awed by our ability to wipe out humanity with a nuclear bomb. Today global warming has exponentially replicated that danger, and humanity must get it right this time around.

- While an "every man for himself" mindset has increasingly defined our industrialized culture, we're actually all in this together.

The crisis succeeded in bringing home to Main Street a single essential point that the corporate responsibility movement had been trying in vain for years to get people from all walks of life to understand: The system that brought us the terrible pain of rising unemployment, a stock market collapse that wiped out trillions of dollars of value for average Americans, and a housing crisis that left millions of families facing foreclosure or worse must give way to the possibility of a new social order. Although the crisis was abysmal, its timing was perfect; it occurred just in time to convince Americans to give a new kind of President a chance to try some new ideas and create what we hope will be a new paradigm embodying a global consciousness committed to "we" not "me" and the universal understanding that this little rock upon which we fly through space is as delicate as it is beautiful.

Now a new day is at hand. And in it we must become the true guardians of the next seven generations. Get ready to do your part because you are needed more now than ever before.

3.4 The Best Examples of Companies That Have Begun To Transform Themselves

The possibilities for the prosperous coexistence of sustainability and capitalism may be best understood through the highly unusual partnership we discussed in Chapter 1 between Nobel Peace Prize winner Muhammad Yunus and Danone, the French food company that built a yogurt factory in Bangladesh. What's so amazing about this story is that Danone believes that profits are not necessarily essential to "always" creating shareholder value. That there are times when it is appropriate to deploy corporate capital in the pursuit of social benefit that will ultimately create additional brand value.

Danone CEO Franck Riboud says his company can see social benefits from its Bangladesh investment and that these may someday be reported on Danone's bottom line right along with the revenue from its many brands. "We're saying that profit maximization is not going to be the only way to measure value," said Emmanuel Faber, Danone's former CFO, in a January 2007 article in Fortune magazine. "There is a whole emerging area of picking stocks for social impact."

Here's more from that article:

"Along a dirt road in Bangladesh's green, fertile heartland, 140 miles northwest of Dhaka, workers in flip-flops are hauling bricks, pouring cement and hammering boards. The object of their labor: a small yogurt factory being built by Danone, the French food company, on the outskirts of Bogra. It may not look like much, but the one-story building behind a wrought-iron gate is the epicenter of a Big New Idea—one that Muhammad Yunus, the winner of the Nobel Peace Prize for his pioneering work on microcredit, thinks can revolutionize a world still being transformed by his first big idea.

"'I hope it will be an important landmark in the annals of business,' Yunus says a few days later in Dhaka, at the opening ceremony for the factory in early November. 'The concept it represents is very powerful.'

"At a lunch in Paris, in the fall of 2005, Yunus invited Danone CEO Franck Riboud to come to Bangladesh and build his first social business enterprise. Riboud listened, then agreed. The yogurt Danone would make would be fortified to help curb malnutrition and priced (at 7 cents a cup) to be affordable. All revenue from the joint venture with Grameen would be reinvested, with Danone taking out only its initial cost of capital, about $500,000, after three years.

"The factory—and ultimately 50 more, if it works—will rely on Grameen microborrowers buying cows to sell it milk on the front end, Grameen microvendors selling the yogurt door to door, and Grameen's 6.6 million members purchasing it for their kids. It will employ 15 to 20 women.

"And Danone estimates that it will provide income for 1,600 people within a 20-mile radius of the plant. Biodegradable cups made from cornstarch, solar panels for electricity generation, and rainwater collection vats make the enterprise environmentally friendly.

"For Riboud the enterprise is about expanding into new markets with nutrition-enhancing products. 'It's really a growth strategy for our company,' he says over a bowl of onion soup in a Dhaka hotel. 'We are convinced that in this world, when you are a consumer-goods company and the country is a developing country, it would be crazy to think only about the peak of the pyramid.'

"But it's clear also that Riboud agrees to a large extent with Yunus's worldview. 'Is the classic economic model working?' he asks. 'No! But I told him, 'I don't want to make charity.' The strength is that it is a business, and if it is a business, it is sustainable. Your shareholders are happy.'"

This is a real breakthrough. If we can harness the experience and financial resources of the world's largest companies to address fundamental issues of equity, justice, and poverty in a sustainable manner, the future will be brighter, and it will arrive quicker than most people can imagine.

On the other side of the world, Jim Rogers, the chairman and chief executive of Duke Energy, is trying to turn his own industry upside down. Rogers is working to transform his company from a cause of global warming into a solution. His idea is called "save-a-watt," and it aims to reward utilities for the energy they save customers via energy efficiency improvements rather than the kilowatts they sell customers by building more power plants.

Thomas Freidman, author of *The World is Flat* and an advocate of the economic benefits of sustainability, recently wrote in his New York Times Op-Ed column:

"Mr. Rogers's proposal is based on three simple principles. The first is that the cheapest way to generate clean, emissions-free power is by improving energy efficiency. Or, as he puts it, 'The most environmentally sound, inexpensive and reliable power plant is the one we don't have to build because we've helped our customers save energy.'

"Second, we need to make energy efficiency something that is as 'back of mind' as energy usage. If energy efficiency depends on people remembering to do 20 things on a checklist, it's not going to happen at scale.

"Third, the only institutions that have the infrastructure, capital, and customer base to empower lots of people to become energy efficient are the utilities, so they are the ones who need to be incentivized to make big investments in efficiency that can be accessed by every customer.

"The only problem is that, historically, utilities made their money by making large-scale investments in new power plants, whether coal or gas or nuclear. As long as a utility could prove to its regulators that the demand for that new plant was there, the utility got to pass along the cost, and then some, to its customers. Mr. Rogers's save-a-watt concept proposes to change all of that.

"'The way it would work is that the utility would spend the money and take the risk to make its customers as energy efficient as possible,' he explained. That would include installing devices in your home that would allow the utility to adjust your air-conditioners or refrigerators at peak usage times. It would include plans to incentivize contractors to build more efficient homes with more efficient boilers, heaters, appliances, and insulation. It could even include partnering with a factory to buy the most energy-efficient equipment or with a family to winterize their house.

"'Energy efficiency is the 'fifth fuel'—after coal, gas, renewables, and nuclear,' said Mr. Rogers. 'Today, it is the lowest-cost alternative and is emissions-free. It should be our first choice in meeting our growing demand for electricity, as well as in solving the climate challenge.'

"Because energy efficiency is, in effect, a resource, he added, in order for utilities to use more of it, 'efficiency should be treated as a production cost in the regulatory arena.' The utility would earn its money on the basis of the actual watts it saves through efficiency innovations. (California's 'decoupling' systems go partly in this direction.)

"At the end of the year, an independent body would determine how many watts of energy the utility has saved over a predetermined baseline and the utility would then be compensated by its customers accordingly.

"'Over time,' said Mr. Rogers, 'the price of electricity per unit will go up, because there would be an incremental cost in adding efficiency equipment—although that cost would be less than the incremental cost of adding a new power plant. But your overall bills should go down, because your home will be more efficient and you will use less electricity.'

"Once such a system is in place, Mr. Rogers added, 'our engineers would wake up every day thinking about how to squeeze more pro-ductivity gains out of new technology for energy efficiency—rather than just how to build a bigger transmission or distribution network to meet the growing demands of customers.' (Why don't we think about incentivizing U.S. automakers the same way—give them tax rebates for save-a-miles?)

"Pulling all this off will be very complicated. But if Mr. Rogers and North Carolina can do it, it would be the mother of all energy para-digm shifts."

My last example of companies transforming themselves can be found much closer to home in a project that Seventh Generation has been involved with since 2006. In this case, a not-for-profit organization has figured out how to create a for-profit business that enables sustainable and systemic change.

Based in Oakland, California, WAGES (Women's Action to Gain Economic Security) creates new jobs and empowers low-income women by organizing and incubating cooperative businesses. WAGES has started three successful environmentally-friendly cleaning cooperatives in the San Francisco Bay Area, and in 2008 some 60 worker-owners served more than 1,000 clients. Coop members earn 50-100% more than is average for clean-ing workers and receive benefits ranging from health, dental, and disability insurance to paid holidays and vacations.

WAGES is using business to do what most people had believed just wasn't possible. The program has successfully demonstrated its ability to enable low-income Latina women to escape poverty and transform their families' lives through the creation of their own businesses.

At a time when our government has totally failed to systemically ad-dress poverty even as it has accelerated a huge transfer of wealth to those who already have more than they need, WAGES has shown the power of the human spirit to rise above the odds that have been placed against it. If our country is ever to fulfill its potential it will only be through capturing the talent and passion of all of its people.

WAGES is offering another benefit to its members and their clients, too. Because they use Seventh Generation's natural, non-toxic cleaning products, not only are they creating healthier homes for their clients, they're no longer experiencing the headaches, rashes, asthma attacks, and other problems that plague people who clean for a living.

I recently had the opportunity to spend an afternoon with several members of the Natural Home Cleaning Coop in Oakland as part of a collaborative effort Seventh Generation is undertaking with WAGES to help them expand their success. Although it may not be the way you'd expect to describe a cleaning worker, these were self-possessed, vibrant professional women. To see the pride and accomplishment on their faces was a truly moving experience.

Veronica, a cooperative owner of the Eco-Care Professional Housecleaning said about her experience, "I am from Guadalajara, Mexico, and I am the mother of two young children. My first pregnancy was difficult, and I did not work. But with my second, I felt safe working because I knew I wasn't using toxic products. I have learned to value my health, and now I only use safe products at home.

"Economically, it has been very helpful to have stability and job security. Before, I worked at McDonalds (earning $5.70 per hour), in a box assembly factory ($6 per hour), and for a commercial housecleaning company ($8 per hour). Now I make $13 an hour, and I have been at Eco-Care for 6 years. As a result, I am more independent. First, I was able to buy a car, and then two months ago, I bought a house in Gilroy!

I like being part of a coop—I know more people and I'm part of a group. Eco-Care is recognized in the community as a business that protects the environment, and that recognition is nice. We share a community with our clients, and they look at us with respect."

Seventh Generation is committed to helping WAGES create cooperative cleaning businesses throughout the United States. The tremendous social returns from this venture require investment in the same way that economic returns do. WAGES provides the initial organizing, training, business systems, support and nurturing that the cooperatives need in order to become self-sustaining businesses. And WAGES can't expand these efforts without assistance.

In February 2009, the fourth cooperative opened under the name, "The Living Home Cleaning Cooperative; A WAGES-Seventh Generation Partnership."

3.5 The Most Important Things We Need To Do

In an April, 2008 speech to the UK Sustainable Development Commission, Herman Daly laid out a plan for reforming the capitalist economy to make it more compatible with a just and sustainable world.

Daly, in introducing his plan, noted, "While these transitional policies will appear radical to many, it is worth remembering that, in addition to being amenable to gradual application, they are based on the conservative institutions of private property and decentralized market allocation. They simply recognize that private property loses its legitimacy if too unequally distributed, and that markets lose their legitimacy if prices do not tell the whole truth about costs. In addition, the macro-economy becomes an absurdity if its scale is structurally required to grow beyond the biophysical limits of the Earth. And well before that radical physical limit we are encountering the conservative economic limit in which extra costs of growth become greater than the extra benefits."

A fitting end to this chapter, here's Daly's plan to get business and our economy where it needs to go:

1. **Cap-auction-trade systems for basic resources**. Cap and trade systems use economic incentives to limit the rate of use of natural resources and the generation of pollution. This system would try and ensure that we did not use natural resources at a rate that is faster that the rate at which they can be regenerated. This would be accomplished by user fees that rise as the rate of extraction rises beyond what is sustainable.

2. **Ecological tax reform**—shift the tax base from value-added taxes (on labor and capital) onto "that to which value is added," namely the resources extracted from nature (depletion) and all the externalities that escape measurement (pollution). By creating a system of "full cost accounting" that internalizes external costs. we will provide more pricing that is more sustainable.

3. **Limit the range of inequality in income distribution**—a minimum income and a maximum income is clearly a radical idea. Poverty reduction now requires some redistribution of wealth. While complete equality of wealth is unfair; unlimited inequality is equally unfair, thus we need to create fair limits to inequality.

4. **Free up the length of the working day, week, and year**—because we need to create some limits on growth we must also allow greater options for leisure and personal work. Full-time employment for all is difficult to provide without unlimited growth, thus we will need to explore increasing a greater balance between work and leisure time. This will likely result in most people working fewer hours so that everyone has the opportunity to work.

7. **Move to 100% reserve requirements** instead of fractional reserve banking. Fractional reserve banking allows financial institutions to leverage limited amounts of capital into hugely leveraged bets. This is in part the problem behind the current financial crisis and at the heart of the "derivatives" problem.

8. **Enclose the remaining commons of rival natural capital** in public trusts, and place a value on these natural resources so that if they are used for commerce they are adequately paid for. While we limit the use of the commons (our fresh water, air, biodiversity, public lands) we must free from private enclosure our commonwealth of knowledge and information, moving beyond access the Internet has provided to the complete democratization of knowledge. Stop treating the scarce (natural resources) as if it were non scarce, and the non scarce (information) as if it were scarce.

9. **Stabilize population.**

Chapter 4
A Brief History of Seventh Generation

4.1 In the Beginning

In 1983, Alan Newman helped launch a retailer called Gardener's Supply Company with his friend Will Raap. The driving idea was that gardening and sustainable agricultural and environmental practices improve communities and can save the planet.

Newman's work at Gardener's Supply led to another start-up called Niche Marketing, a catalog fulfillment company servicing small progressive organizations who couldn't afford to run their own warehouses and customer service operations. One of Niche Marketing's clients was Renew America, a Washington, DC-based environmental group selling energy efficient lighting and water conservation products.

Unfortunately for Renew America, sales were a dud. "This was in 1988, really before the environmental movement took off," Newman said. "Renew America kept offering the business to me, and I kept saying, 'No, thank you.' The catalog was awful, the product selection was awful, and I didn't believe there was enough market. When they said they were going to throw it in the garbage can if I didn't do it, the word 'OK' came out of my mouth. We changed the catalog, the products, the name, and frankly, the world changed, which had more to do with it than my great vision. And I think it was three to six months afterward that Jeff came on board."

I had called Alan after having written about the catalog in my book, *How to Make the World a Better Place*. As I checked the facts prior to publication, I learned that the catalog was about to go under. When I asked if I could help, Newman said he needed someone to raise money. So I wrote a business plan and raised $850,000 from a pool of private investors, who had previously enjoyed a huge return on their investment in the Network for Learning, a business that I'd started and ultimately sold to Warner Communications. In exchange, I made one of the best deals of my life: I became an equal owner of Seventh Generation.

Under the deal, Alan and I would each own 23% of company stock. There were about 40 other shareholders, none of whom would own more than 3%. I continued to live in New York City and commuted to Vermont a few days a week where I primarily focused on finance and product development. Alan oversaw marketing and day-to-day operations.

All we needed was a better name. As you can imagine, Niche Marketing didn't really capture the spirit of our new company's mission to help people reduce their impact on our environment and make the planet a better place for our children and grandchildren.

An employee of Mohawk Native American descent suggested we take our name from the Great Law of the Haudenosaunee (the Six Nations Iroquois Confederacy), an ancient document which instructed its people that "in our every deliberation, we must consider the impact of our decisions on the next seven generations."

This Native American quote quite eloquently expressed the idea that our ecosystems are fragile and delicate places only temporarily entrusted to our care and reflected the concern that our actions have repercussions that can affect many future generations. We liked it, it stuck, and to this day Seventh Generation honors this founding philosophy by developing and marketing products which represent environmentally superior alternatives to products that are generally available, which makes it possible for our customers to become part of a solution to the problems facing our planet.

4.2 A Quick Look at the Great Law

The founding document of the oldest living participatory democracy on Earth, the Great Law of the Haudenosaunee is one of humanity's most important texts. Along with the Magna Carta, it was one of the key inspirations for our country's own constitution.

The Great Law was created in the late 16th century when five northern Iroquois tribes—the Cayugas, Mohawks, Onondagas, Oneidas, and Senecas, living in what is now New York State, joined together to form the League of the Iroquois. Translating as "We Are Of the Extended Lodge," the name "Haudenosaunee" symbolizes the unity of the tribes.

Before the formulation of the League, the five tribes were in a state of constant warfare among themselves. Recognizing the need for an end to the hostilities, Deganawideh, a visionary prophet, and Hiawatha, an accomplished orator, embarked upon a mission to heal the divisions between the tribes. After years of negotiations, they forged an alliance among the Iroquois nations, based on Deganawideh's far-reaching vision. The Great Law of Peace, as it came to be known, revitalized the tribes by organizing them into matriarchal clans and emphasizing equality, consent of the governed, and above all, peace.

Since Deganawideh's time, the Great Law of the Haudenosaunee has been passed down orally from generation to generation. Four hundred years later, the Great Law of Peace still resonates powerfully, and the Iroquois nation continues to operate on the original model and its principles of equality and justice. The Great Law expresses the humanity of the Iroquois people, and we feel it embodies the philosophy we must all embrace to make the world a better place.

Over the years many people have suggested we consider changing our name to something that provides a clearer and more obvious description of what we do, but we have resisted the temptation. (Think Eco, Planet Friendly, Green Products, or Enviro-Logic.) Our name, while complex and challenging (like everything else about us!), has a beautiful rich heritage and a deeply resonant meaning we will spend the rest of our lives trying to live up to.

4.3 A Seventh Generation Timeline

1988–1989: A New Kind of Company is Born

In 1988, The non-profit organization Renew America hands its failing mail order catalog over to Niche Marketing Services, a contract fulfillment house for progressive mail order catalogs started in 1985 by Alan Newman at Gardener's Supply Company in Burlington, Vermont. Alan has resisted taking over the catalog, but agrees to give it a second chance rather than let it simply die.

In 1989, I partner with Alan Newman to raise funding for the business, which is renamed Seventh Generation. Sales grow steadily from $100,000 in 1988 to $7 million in 1990, the 20th anniversary of Earth Day. The most popular product, French string shopping bags, are backordered for over a year. The company receives about 500,000 phone calls in 1990 from people requesting a copy of our catalog. All is well and spirits are high.

1990–1994: The Terrible Teens
(Surviving Adolescence By the Skin of Our Laundry Liquid)

In 1990, with new money from a second round of financing, the company moves to new space in nearby Colchester near the current location of Costco and adjacent to a medical waste incinerator that has since been shut down. Alan quickly transforms it into a cheerful hippy den. There is a ping-pong table in the warehouse, free Ben & Jerry's filling an industrial freezer in the company kitchen, and chalkboards in the bathrooms where people can write things about the company they don't feel comfortable saying out loud.

The main conference room, where we hold staff meetings, has no table or chairs. Only pillows. No matter how busy the company is, Alan insists on weekly "check-ins" at which every employee is invited to report on new projects, problems, or just about anything else. Some stick to business, others discuss conflicts with co-workers or troubles at home. The idea is to create a culture of absolute honesty in which employees would not be hampered by fear of admitting mistakes or suffering disapproval. Alan is clearly the driver of this culture—though I have spent my life as an entrepreneur, I am at this point more comfortable in a suit and tie, seated at a conference room table.

I keep a small office in midtown Manhattan with an assistant and a staff of about five. Alan and I speak on the phone several times a day. While the office culture in Vermont is very different than the one I might have created, I adapt—sitting in beanbag chairs without complaint, though I do conduct my own meetings in a smaller conference room outfitted with a more traditional table and chairs.

Anticipating continued exponential growth, the company continues to expand and reaches a total of 120 employees. Then the Earth Day bubble bursts. Sales, which were expected to be $21 million in 1991, end up at only $7 million. Led by Peter Hollender, my brother, the wholesale business is born in an effort to generate additional sales. Seventh Generation's first retail store opens on Battery Street in Burlington and is managed by John Quinney, the former executive director of the New Alchemy Institute.

The business begins a series of huge operating losses running into millions of dollars. (The company would not become profitable for another decade.) These loses create an environment of endless stress and constant crisis.

At this point, Seventh Generation has the overhead, debt, and equity of a $20 million business but nowhere near the sales. Worse yet, we are mailing millions of catalogs a year at a cost of $1.25 each to people who just aren't buying. I go into survival mode, cutting expenses as fast as I can.

We go from 120 employees to 60. We renegotiate everything. Our lease, the copying machine, our warehouse equipment. If we have to pay for it, we have to renegotiate the cost to survive. At this point, Alan is truly miserable and wants to take some time off.

He takes the layoffs particularly hard and isn't sure how to proceed. We have hit a wall and must reinvent ourselves. I am burnt out but I've been through this before. Quitting is not an option for me. Alan says he needs time to think things through. At the beginning of 1992, he tells me that he will be taking a six-month sabbatical. I am furious. I feel Alan is abandoning me. I think, 'If you're leaving now, don't bother coming back.' To make matters worse, my brother Peter decides to leave the business at the same time.

Alan and I had already begun to harbor deep differences about the company's direction. Despite the slumping sales, Alan remains confident in the catalog business. I, on the other hand, believe that Seventh Generation's true potential lies in becoming a full-scale consumer brand. My goal is to narrow the company's range of products to popular items like recycled bathroom tissue paper, mass-produce them, and retail everything under the Seventh Generation label.

Alan and I have a very hard falling out. We don't talk to each other for years.

In 1992, when Alan wants to return to the business, the Board of Directors and I decide that we should part ways permanently. Peter Graham, a grade school friend of mine, purchases Alan's stock, which provides the seed capital for his new business, The Magic Hat Brewing Company.

1992 is also the year that Bill Clinton was running against George H.W. Bush for the presidency. I feel strongly enough about the election to use the cover of the catalog for an unflattering cartoon of Bush and his Republican cohorts; with big grins on their faces, they are pictured using poisonous aerosol sprays, approving clear-cutting, dripping with oil, and denying the existence of an ozone hole in the earth's atmosphere. Inside the catalog we wrote an impassioned essay asking people to "Vote for the Earth!"

The catalog cover ends up being a $250,000 contribution to the Democratic party—we lose that much in orders. For many years I count this decision as one of the biggest mistakes I ever made. I was terrified about what would happen to the country if Clinton and Gore didn't get elected. I wasn't sure I even wanted to continue to live here in the US. We thought we had made a careful case for why it was important for us as a business to take a political stand and that our focus on an environmentally-driven agenda made our foray into electoral waters acceptable.

Our customers think otherwise. They don't want the company that sells them toilet paper to tell them how to vote. It's outside the relationship we have established with them. I am shocked that so many people are upset and angry. I thought we would get lots of positive remarks for being brave and courageous and up front. But mostly we hear negative comments.

By the end of 1992, Seventh Generation is stabilized. In 1993, we're back to breaking even. But we still need capital.

By 1993, I have run out of family members, friends, associates, doctors, dentists, mailmen, milkmen, and random strangers I can convince to invest in the company. As a last resort, unwilling to take funds from venture capital firms, we take Seventh Generation public at $5.00 a share. Thousands of people respond. Most of them are unfortunately motivated by the belief that they will make a quick buck. Yet if they read the materials the SEC insists we provide, they'll know how unlikely that is.

1995–1999: Growing Up and Moving On

The wholesale business takes off on the coattails of well-timed dramatic growth in the natural food industry in general and Whole Foods in particular. Whole Foods needs more products that they could possibly find to fill their massive stores, and so Seventh Generation ends up with a whole aisle of its own. In many respects Whole Foods is the engine that not only saves us, but puts our company and brand in front of the hundreds of thousands of customers that today form the Seventh Generation Nation.

In 1995, the catalog business, which had never made a dime in profit, is sold to Gaiam, a new company founded by Yirka Rysevy, the founder of office supply giant Corporate Express. Yirka is convinced that if people find out that he is diverting his attention away from his responsibilities at Corporate Express, they will sell their stock causing its price to plummet and investors to lose hundreds of millions of dollars. He shows up at our offices to inspect his acquisition in a disguise (I swear I am not making this up!). Yirka is known as an unusual corporate CEO. He lives in the hills high above Boulder, Colorado in a small cabin with no electricity or running water. I can't understand why someone so concerned with leading such a simple life holds all his meetings with me at the Four Seasons hotel.

Gaiam becomes a significant wholesale customer and licenses the Seventh Generation name for $100,000 a year to use on its mail order catalog for the next three years before it is renamed Harmony. Without the sale of the catalog and the subsequent revenue from Gaiam, it's unlikely that Seventh Generation would have survived.

With the sale of our catalog, the company focuses exclusively on building its wholesale brand in natural food stores.

In 1999, with the help of Peter Graham, Seventh Generation buys back all of the stock it had sold to the public in 1993 for $1.30 a share, a 40% premium over the $.84 price at which the stock has been trading. As a private company we are suddenly free of the conditions and restrictions placed on publicly-owned entities. We are also safe from the possibility that some unanticipated investor would try to purchase the company out from under us in a hostile takeover bid.

It's at this point that Seventh Generation also changes its tag line from "Products for a Healthy Planet" to "Safer for You and the Environment."

This change mirrors a change we're making to our product positioning in order to better reflect the buying motivation of our rapidly growing consumer base and respond to a seismic shift in market trends.

Organic foods, which once had occupied the same quiet retail backwater as natural household products, are suddenly selling in mainstream grocery stores. But it is consumers' lifestyle and health concerns, not their concerns for the environment, that are driving this enormous change. People aren't buying organic apples because they're worried about polluting streams. They're worried about consuming pesticides and getting cancer. When consumer research reveals these and many other similar motivations, we begin to focus on issues like asthma, allergies, and chemical sensitivity, all of which can be exacerbated by common household cleaners that contain chemicals like chlorine, petrochemicals, and volatile organic compounds.

This repositioning changes the course of our business. For the first time since 1990, sales begin to grow rapidly, nearly tripling from just over $3 million in 1995 to nearly $9 million in 1998.

2000–2005: The Industry Leader For a New Millennium

Crunchy granola environmentalists and body-conscious New-agers collide with aging baby boomers to create a health and wellness awareness tsunami that lifts Seventh Generation to new heights of success. In many important respects the current era of our company begins in 2000, the first year we are once again a private company. Responding to this exploding market, Seventh Generation builds the infrastructure to become a leading distributor to the health food channel and begins an expansion into traditional supermarkets.

From 2000 to 2005, sales grow steadily as does the value of the company's stock. By 2005 Seventh Generation offers over 70 branded products and is the leading marketer of natural, non-toxic household products in the United States. According to SPINscan data for the natural foods industry, the company's market share for the 52-week period ending September 10, 2005 is 45% of the total sales in the paper and plastic, cleaning, diaper, wipes, and feminine hygiene categories. (Broken out by category this translates into a 56% share in the paper and plastic category; a 37% share in the cleaning products category; and a 53% share in the diapers, wipes, and feminine hygiene category.)

The Company's gross sales have grown from $3.2 million in 1995 to almost $50 million in 2005. This represents an average compounded growth rate of 31.6% per year, a pace that's more than double that of the Natural Products Industry as a whole, which varying estimates place somewhere between 8–12% a year.

In 2002, after 14 years of losing money, the company enjoys its very first profitable year of operations. Much credit goes to Jeff Phillips, who for almost 10 years has relentlessly tried to convince me that making money is not a bad or evil thing. To this day, he saves an article sent to him in which I affirm my epiphany about how much better life is going to be once we start making money.

In 2003 we publish our first corporate responsibility report. This is a highly controversial decision. My newfound passion for talking about everything we are doing wrong is met with concern if not outright fear on the part of our management team. They are sure that our meditation on our faults and shortcomings will be used by our competitors to our disadvantage.

This trepidation is largely my own creation. Though I had spent many months reading everything I could find on CSR reporting, I had not invited the company or its management team along on my journey. When I excitedly announce the project, I use what in hindsight is a very poor choice of words to describe the endeavor. We would be publishing a report, I say, that, "highlights everything that is wrong with the products we sell along with all the other things that are wrong with the company." People think I've gone crazy. After a few months of dialogue and education, my passion prevails, but not without much hesitation on the part of almost everyone else involved.

In the end, we produce a report we're not afraid for the world to see. Here's an example of the kind of transparency it provides:

"While we are tremendously proud of what we have accomplished, some of our products are not as authentic to our environmental mission as we would like them to be. We sometimes have to make trade-offs between environmental benefits, product performance, and product cost. We have prepared a critique of our own products to deepen understanding around some of the choices and trade-offs we have made relative to specific product ingredients. It may seem a bit unusual that we've chosen to critique our own products, but we believe that a key part of being a socially responsible business is transparency—and that means sharing what's really going on, not just what we'd like people to see."

The report also notes:

"We are committed to creating an exceptional workplace community, one that inspires honesty and trust, respect and compassion, and a spirited sense of play. A community that provides opportunities for growth and the freedom to realize our full potential."

Our report lays out those things about our products and our company that we think still need some work. And while there are indeed one or two instances of our competitors using our report against us, our fearless leadership into the brave new world of corporate transparency lays the foundation for what is to become a fundamentally important strategic advantage.

In 2004, my third book, *What Matters Most: How a Small Group of Pioneers Is Teaching Social Responsibility to Big Business, and Why Big Business Is Listening* is published to critical raves and very few readers. While I never make it onto the bestseller lists, the book contemplates the importance of corporate responsibility for our society and is an important part of my journey.

In 2005 the company expands into the diaper business, which is probably our most important product introduction in the last decade. Our brown diaper, an aesthetic decision I make in the face of many disbelievers, will turn out to lay the foundation for our most important buyer class, new moms. The value of company stock soars from \$2.00 in 2000 to \$10.00 in 2005.

Perhaps most importantly, In 2005 we also write a new vision statement for the company that says our goal is to create "a society whose guiding principles include environmental sustainability, social justice, and compassion for all living creatures; and an earth that is restored, protected, and cherished for this generation and those to come."

Sometime around September of 2005, we finally get around to publishing our 2004 corporate responsibility report. My opening letter is titled "Redefining Reality." It speaks of my perspective on the state of our company, reporting in general, and the world at large:

> "Consciously or unconsciously, we all choose the lens through which we frame the world.... At Seventh Generation, we aspire to widen the lens to more fully understand the inter-relationship and interdependence of all things, and thus our own responsibility and impact as a company. We want to understand how choices about the ingredients in our products and the bottles and boxes we put them in affect the environment. We want to know how the practices of our suppliers and distributors affect the communities where our products are sold. We strive to grasp how the way we treat our employees ripples out into the world. Understanding those complex relationships necessi-

tates open and honest dialogue—with our employees, customers, and other stakeholders. It means creating a safe environment in which tough and complex questions can be asked, one in which dissent and self-expression are encouraged, one in which we're willing to hear (and act on) harsh criticism."

It is our hope that our report will raise the bar for ourselves as well as other businesses. Yet it remains unclear if anyone is actually reading the report let alone taking it to heart. That's why we're heartened to learn that our 2004 corporate responsibility report is selected by the Ceres-ACCA North American Awards for Sustainability Reporting as the Best Small or Medium Enterprise Report. Ceres calls it "a pioneering effort in transparency for a privately owned company."

Beyond our office walls, things are changing as well. In February of 2005, nine months before I meet with Wal-Mart CEO Lee Scott for the first time, Scott himself meets with over eighty institutional members of the Interfaith Center on Corporate Responsibility (ICCR). They raise concerns about Wal-Mart's business model and explain the necessity of socially responsible business practices, including environmental accountability, and the amelioration of the retailing giant's negative impacts on those regions of the world where its products are manufactured. Not convinced that Wal-Mart is headed in the right direction, several shareholder resolutions are put forward by ICCR members requesting that Wal-Mart produce reports on its sustainability practices, equal employment opportunities, and distribution of equity compensation. Two years later, Wal-Mart will commit to begin to report on these issues, something that is inconceivable at the time.

By 2005 the Global Compact, a United Nations sponsored initiative to encourage corporate responsibility launched in January 1999 by then Secretary-General Kofi Annan, has 2,000 participants from over 70 countries. This is an important milestone but it is nonetheless a small figure when compared to the 60,000+ transnational corporations that currently do business in more than one country and smaller still when you consider that this initiative requires only "voluntary" changes and that there is absolutely no means of accountability to ensure that any of the signatory companies have actually made any of the changes to which they've committed.

This history is compiled in part from stories that appeared in Vermont Business Magazine (12/04), INC. Magazine (10/04), and NRDC's On Earth (11/04).

Chapter 5

Seventh Generation's Mid-Life Crisis: Redefining Purpose & Possibility

In 2004, our CSR reporting labors finally bore fruit in the form of some significant national recognition. One such honor was one of the greatest I think our company has ever received simply because it came from the heart of the traditional business community.

Picture this:

I'm two blocks from the White House at the headquarters of the US Chamber of Commerce, an organization to which we've never belonged and with whose local chamber we have frequently clashed. I'm sitting in the famous International Hall of Flags at table number one with Secretary of Commerce Don Evans. Also at the table is Raymond Gilmartin, President & CEO of the Merck pharmaceutical company and Robert Nardelli, President of Home Depot. Also seated at my table is Michael Novak, a public policy scholar at the American Enterprise Institute, one of America's most conservative "think tanks." There's not a single person in this whole room that I've ever met before.

What is Seventh Generation doing here?

As one of four finalists for the Small Business Corporate Stewardship Awards, we are being honored by the traditional business establishment as one of the best examples of small business corporate citizenship in the entire nation.

And we win.

Seventh Generation, an outlier in the corporate world and an aspiring leader of the corporate responsibility movement, is actually recognized as the best example of corporate citizenship around, an honor based on our "demonstration of ethical leadership and corporate stewardship, making a difference in (our) communities, and contributions to the advancement of important economic and social goals."

That may have been the most remarkable recognition we received in 2004, but it was no means the only honor we were given.

That year we also won the 2004 Veggie Award which was given by VegNews, America's premier vegetarian lifestyle magazine. We were named one of the Top 10 Responsible Brands in America. We were selected as one of the Fast 50 by Fast Company Magazine. And we were chosen as one of New England's Best Workplaces for Commuters and honored by the Minnesota-based Alliance for Sustainability for the greatest accomplishment across a wide range of sustainability endeavors.

That year I also personally received the Terry Ehrich Award "for having created a business model that encompasses a healthy and productive workplace, welcomes and promotes flexibility for employees, and has a key focus on the importance of life-friendly policies."

But between the awards we were getting and the incredible growth we were experiencing lay a question we never seemed able to answer: Where was all this headed? What should our business accomplish over the next 3, 5, or even 10 years? We were unwittingly operating on the time-tested principle that says if you don't know where you're going any road will get you there. We knew we needed a strategic plan, but no one at the company had ever created one, so we went in search of a "consultant."

We found an incredible partner in a man named Scott Lutz, who agreed to create a plan for us. As this profile in the May 2002 issue of Fast Company magazine suggests, Scott seemed like the perfect match for us:

"Scott Lutz looks the part of the corporate pioneer, what with his faded denim shirt, gray woolly vest, cords, Skechers, and just the right amount of facial hair. Around his neck is a talisman, awarded at one of his company's regular gatherings. The thin leather strip, looped into two figure-eight knots, is adorned with a stamped metal dog tag, eight ivory beads to signify his company's core values, and a lone crimson bead for courage. 'I got the red one because my team said nobody but me would have the guts to stand up and defend the name '8th Continent' in front of the board,' he says, laughing.

"Lutz, 43, is president and CEO of 8th Continent, a young soy-milk company that is headquartered out of Minnetonka, Minnesota. But don't get the wrong idea. Lutz and his colleagues aren't some fringy whole-earth startup. Their company is a 50-50 joint venture between two corporate giants, DuPont and General Mills, and their target is a fast-growing segment of the food business. Lutz says that 8th Continent aims to combine 'the power of the big with the spirit of the small'—to create a fresh new brand (and a nimble new company) using the technology and financial resources of two major players."

Scott had worked at Proctor & Gamble before his soy beverage venture. He understood branding and corporate strategy, and talked about building our tiny company into a billion dollar business. It sounded exciting. Unfortunately, halfway through the process, I had the startling realization that while Scott was creating an amazing strategic plan, it was for a company at which I wouldn't want to work! It was for a company that had incredible growth potential but none of the heart and soul that found me jumping out of bed every morning eager to get to the office. So we said goodbye to Scott. The question of who we wanted to be when we grew up remained unanswered. And we continued to operate on our time-tested principle of taking whatever road we found ourselves upon at the moment.

For my part, I was beginning to wonder if I was the right person to lead the company through its next stage of growth. I questioned whether I had a vision that was compelling enough or could provide the leadership that the business needed to fulfill it. I was also pretty tired, stressed out, and uncertain about what I wanted to do with the rest of my life. With these issues unresolved, we pushed on.

From the outside things couldn't have looked better. In 2005, our sales reached $49 million, growing 37% over the prior year. Not only were we making money and growing rapidly, we were receiving a wave of recognition for our corporate responsibility work, acclaim that cemented our leadership position within the field.

While our purpose seemed obvious to outsiders, inside the company it wasn't at all clear. In an effort to be inclusive and embrace the various ideas of the whole team, the company had increasingly begun to pursue many different directions at once, some of which were in direct conflict with others. Growth, profitability, education, advocacy, developing consumer products, being a model of corporate responsibility, creating the best place to work, saving the planet, making the world a better place. This was our agenda, and the company couldn't effectively do it all at the same time.

A year after our first attempt to create a strategic plan failed, we were ready to try again. In the spring of 2005 a group of about 16 people that we ultimately named the "Change Leadership Team," met with a woman named Carol Sanford. Carol was about as different from Scott Lutz as you could imagine. She was a short, jovial, lady who exuded so much warmth and passion that it was hard to even imagine her in a room with traditional corporate executives. She convinced us that we shouldn't have ever considered hiring someone to create a strategic plan for us, that we ourselves were the only ones who could create a plan that would truly reflect the essence of who we are and what we believed in. Carol said she would teach us everything we needed to know to do this and that she would work with us as long as we were happy with the work she was doing. We were excited. Carol seemed to really get us, and that in and of itself was a breakthrough.

Carol was a consultant to both Fortune 500 and new economy businesses. Her clients included some companies that Seventh Generation considered part of an evil empire of sorts, firms like DuPont, Weyerhaeuser, Clorox, Colgate Palmolive, Warner-Lambert, Frito-Lay, Hunt-Wesson, Scott Paper, Boeing Commercial Aircraft, and the Ford Motor Company. Carol had over 25 years of global experience helping businesses and organizations strategically position themselves in their markets as indispensable, build developmental leaders that grow people as they execute strategy, and redesign structures, systems, and processes of the operation to embed strategically focused regenerative practices into daily work. We were definitely ready for her help.

With Carol's help, we began a three-phase process:

- Phase I: Establish Seventh Generation's strategic direction
- Phase II: Develop the leadership that all of us will exercise to ensure that we move in an aligned fashion and achieve results
- Phase III: Operationalize the strategy, which includes the re-design of all Seventh Generation processes and systems

In a later chapter, we'll discuss the details of this process, the value we received, as well as the frustration that ensued. While my commitment never wavered, virtually none of the objectives we identified were met on schedule. We pushed on anyway. Instead of developing a strategic plan, we focused on formalizing our values and culture. After 18 years of evolving who we were and what we believed in, it was difficult to bring discipline and focus to our mission and vision. In the sensitive and inclusive culture we had created, we found it very awkward and uncomfortable to articulate what we *weren't* going to be.

As we began to redefine ourselves, Carol led us through a seemingly infinite series of exercises that were designed to help us think about ourselves and our business in new and different ways. We were developing a higher level of consciousness about the way we worked, the way we thought about who we wanted to be, what would be required to fulfill the lofty goals we had set for ourselves, and what would be asked of the participants who signed up for the adventure.

As you'll see, it was not easy. Frankly, it was like slogging through an endless series of swamps. Carol had the map. We didn't, and it often felt like we were stuck in the TV series "Lost."

Chapter 6
Clarity Emerges: Essence, Global Imperatives & Managing Principles

---

6.1 Getting There

2006 was an exceptionally important year for Seventh Generation. As sales reached $63 million, a 28% increase over 2005, we generated an operating income of $1.8 million, a 106% increase over the prior year. This honestly amazed me; I couldn't quite believe that we'd actually made a profit of over one million dollars. It was something that never seemed to matter to me, but at the same time I realized that it was a huge affirmation that our often unusual way of doing business had led not only to terrific growth but was now actually making what felt like a lot of money.

2006 was also a year that I found clarity and a renewed sense of purpose both for myself and for Seventh Generation. I knew for the first time in my life that I had found what I would spend the rest of my life doing. This truth emerged from the process that Carol Sanford led, an amazing combination of academic study, personal development, spiritual journey, and group therapy that was anything but a linear process.

The work taught us to use a series of frameworks in our daily office life, structures that help organize our thinking and doing. The collective use of these frameworks helped us "think together" in a more aligned and purposeful manner.

We also learned to share a series of practices. One that we began to use quite often was called a "task cycle." This was a game plan for organizing a meeting or a project that forced everyone to think in advance about the purpose of what we were about to do, the products that we would create, the effect we hoped to have, how we would go about doing it, and what would be changed in each of us as a result.

All of this embraced a discipline called "systems thinking" that was popularized by Peter Senge in his book, *The Fifth Discipline*. (For more on systems thinking, see Chapter 8) Systems thinking helps us think in a holistic (if not holographic!) way rather than in an isolated, compartmentalized manner. While Senge deserves much credit for bringing this vital idea into the mainstream, Carol taught us what she calls "regenerative systems thinking," a mode of thought that focuses on the upper levels of consciousness and requires personal development for success.

Under Carol's leadership, we also worked through a process that created clarity about who we were (our "essence") and developed the vision that we as a business were uniquely capable of doing which the world needed most (our "global imperatives"). These concepts replaced what most businesses call their mission and vision. We also established a "corporate direction" that provided focus and boundaries for moving between our essence and our global imperatives.

What emerged were new capabilities for looking at, thinking about, perceiving, and understanding the world, our business, and ourselves. It was tough work. It seemed like we were being taught ten times more than we could fully understand let alone use. We all learned at different paces and in different ways The process often left more than a few of us dazed and confused, and we lost several participants along the way.

The most difficult challenge we faced was translating the process to and for the rest of the staff. And it was one to which we usually failed to adequately rise. It took almost three years for us to decide that the best way to ensure everyone was on the same page was to have company-wide development days with everyone in the same room learning at the same time and sharing both their excitement and frustrations.

But no matter what we did (and will continue to do) to make the path clearer and less frustrating, it was (and always will be) murky and challenging. This is simply the nature of journeys to any undiscovered destination. Machete in hand, you have traveled off the edge of the map and are blazing a trail into the unknown. Such an experience will always be marked by fear and confusion but also, hopefully, by a welcome glimpse of enlightenment here and there.

The team that initially engaged in the process with Carol consisted of just 14 people who were then obligated to teach what we were learning to the other 41 people on our staff. Over a period of three years we went from this so called "core team," to an even larger team of 18, then down to a smaller team of just 7 in 2007, which we called the "strategy team."

My experience during this process is well represented by the book *Presence*. Written by Peter M. Senge, C. Otto Scharmer, Joseph Jaworski, and Betty Sue Flowers, *Presence* describes how most of our life experiences fall within the pre-established patterns we seem to follow over and over. Whether it's how we respond to each other, read the newspaper, participate in a meeting, or watch a sunset, most of what we do we do as we have done before. For whatever reason, the possibility of doing it differently doesn't occur to us. Yet it is outside these patterns that all possibility lies. Whether it's figuring out how to stop global warming, be a better lover, or design a new product, 99% of what is possible but yet to be waits in behavioral territory we rarely if ever visit.

If we can slow down our thinking enough to actually watch how we think, become conscious of the generation of our thoughts, question whether there is another way to see what we are seeing, do what we are doing, or hold what we are holding, a whole new world opens up to us.

Presence in many ways captures the ideas and the experience of the process Carol Sanford led us through. Though both the book and the process have unique essential qualities, *Presence* offers someone who has not shared the journey with us a window into what that journey felt like. It is a book that I highly recommend.

6.2 The Essence of Seventh Generation

In many respects, the essence of Seventh Generation is a reflection of my own. So to understand this company's "soul" I started with my own inner exploration. Carol has a structure for understanding essence that is comprised of a core process, a core value, and a core purpose. All three are linked and cannot be wholly understood alone. While others have developed structures that vary and may even compliment Carol's, we used hers since she was our chosen teacher. As you will notice, Carol likes threes. And in almost everything she does, you'll find that number or multiples of it playing an important role.

To see essence, one needs to look for the themes that show up in a recurring fashion throughout one's life. Carol guided me through several conversations in which I told stories about the most meaningful and important parts of my life.

I left my Park Avenue home on the Upper East Side of Manhattan at the age of 17 because (at least in part) of the guilt I felt about being "rich," Or as I was taught to say, "upper middle class." The proposition of having so much when so many others had so little made no sense to me. After driving to Santa Barbara, I lived in my car and worked every day after school rather than take money from my parents. When I was 19, having dropped out of college after three semesters, I studied in London with R.D. Lang to try and understand why our society places sanity and madness at opposite ends of the mental health spectrum.

At 20, having moved to Toronto to live with a woman I had met in college, I started the Skills Exchange because Ivan Illich's book, *Deschooling Society*, had convinced me that educational institutions do more to inhibit the flow of information than they do to provide access to it to people who want to learn. The Skills Exchange organized people from all walks of life and connected them with individuals who wanted to study with them. In homes, offices, the kitchens of restaurants, and even on park benches, people learned everything from poetry to Marxist philosophy and alternative ways to care for diabetes.

I talked to Carol about my anger towards our system of taxation, which effectively takes money from the poor and gives it to the rich. I spoke of my frustration that though we have the ability to produce enough food, people still go hungry. I talked about my distaste for a world that teaches people they are powerless rather than how to use the power they have. I discussed my contempt for a health care system that cures illness rather than preventing it.

I described the pain I felt when my brother passed away in his early 40s. He was always my closest friend. In his death I saw how as he cut his life short, I was wasting too much of my time, time that I would never again recapture. And I saw how my general unconsciousness, the way I so often live waiting for the future to arrive or feeling remiss about the past—rather than living in the present—causes life to pass us by with such speed.

Based on these and other experiences, we defined my core process, the way I see and want to work in the world, as *reconciling systemic dissonance*. This process focuses on the dysfunctional systems that govern the way the world works, and works toward bringing them closer together.

My core process is driven by an obsessive focus on things that make no sense to me on a systemic level, things like the disparity between rich and poor, the way we define sanity and insanity, a health care system that prefers to treat illness (and poorly at that!) rather than prevent it, food production that exceeds our needs but still leaves millions starving.

This revelation meant that the heart and soul of Seventh Generation would center around on uncovering and reconciling the dissonant systems that were most relevant to our business. Something we describe as "systemic dissonance."

Take, for example, the system that subsidizes the cost of many traditional products while artificially increasing the price of natural, organic, and environmental products. This is a classic case of "externalizing costs." It takes elements of the traditional food production process (the pollution of groundwater resulting from the use of pesticides, the adverse health impact on farm workers exposed to the same pesticides, the loss of topsoil, etc.) and excludes those costs from the price of the product. Those costs are instead borne by society as a whole rather than factored into the final price of the food, whether it's a head of lettuce or a pound of beef.

As a result, organic produce, which doesn't require these negative effects, appears more expensive, but only because we fail to charge the farmer producing the conventional food with the full costs of production. Thus, in this system, the healthiest and safest products end up being more expensive than products that are less so. This is an example of systemic dissonance.

Compounding this problem is its chief unintended side effect: The healthiest and safest products are only affordable to the wealthiest consumers. Lower income individuals, who are arguably most in need of safe and healthy products, are the least able to afford them. In this system, Seventh Generation ends up selling its "natural & non-toxic" products to more affluent and correspondingly well-educated consumers.

Other instances of "systemic dissonance" include the system that allows household cleaning products to avoid having to disclose their ingredients to consumers, a fact which makes it difficult for people to choose products that don't contain toxic and carcinogenic chemicals. Another example is the system that concentrates most corporate wealth in the hands of shareholders and senior management rather than the employees that actually create the majority of that value.

There's no shortage of systemic dissonance in today's world. The challenge lies in selecting which issues to work on and in the struggle to develop strategies that meaningfully resolve what are usually huge, pervasive problems.

My core value is more predictable and straightforward than my core process and was much easier to see. It's focused on honesty, transparency, and authenticity, which is much of what my last book, *What Matters Most*, was all about. It means telling everyone the same story and revealing both the good and the bad. It's why if a friend doesn't tell me the truth, I am relentlessly unforgiving. It's why when I speak publicly, I take an almost perverse pleasure in disclosing all the things I am doing wrong.

Many people say that what's most unique about Seventh Generation is its authenticity. But authenticity is a process and a journey, not a state of being. Nothing is totally "authentic." While we've spent 20 years as a company "practicing" authenticity, it's our failures and mistakes as much as our successes that make us authentic. Even more importantly, it's our willingness to publicly reveal and discuss these failures and mistakes that make us authentic. Most of us have learned that it's good to be right, but in truth, we are wrong much of the time. Authenticity is uncharted territory for many people and most businesses. Seventh Generation aspires to be a pioneer in the journey towards authenticity

I have defined both my own and the company's core value as living authentically. Hopefully you've already begun to experience this commitment as you learn about Seventh Generation and my own passions.

My core purpose is to strive to create enlightened justice and equity. It's integrally linked to systemic dissonance and authenticity and has been evident for much of my life. It was there at the age of 15 when I demonstrated in Washington, DC against the war in Vietnam. It was there when I wrote my first book, *How to Make the World a Better Place* and found the chapter on justice and human rights to be the one that mattered most to me. It's there in Seventh Generation's work with WAGES.

Justice and equity are not something that business is very good at. In important respects, it goes against the grain found in capitalism's hyper-competitive, winner-take-all playing field. Justice and equity are not something that Seventh Generation has been very good at either. But, as we have learned from our understanding of sustainability, it is essential that we continue to try until we get it right because justice and equity are not only about poverty and wealth. They are about access to high quality health care and education. They are about not locating the most toxic factories in the poorest neighborhoods. They are about setting a minimum wage that allows a family to live a decent and proud life and ensuring that women are paid comparable to men for the same work. They are about many, many things.

Our efforts to address justice and equity must start right here inside our own company. Is our ownership and compensation structure equitable? Is representation in important decisions fair and just? Too often we look "outside" our own situations when we think about equity and justice rather than starting with that which is closest to home: the relationships we have with each other, our business partners, and our customers and consumers.

We have enjoyed some small external successes in making the world a more equitable and just place. Four projects with which we're involved hold the potential to fulfill our vision of what's possible where equity and justice are concerned. The first is a project to source essential oils from sustainable, cooperative or family owned farms that are growers of organic, non-endangered plants and trees. This type of sourcing is known as fair trade, and it is a critically important strategy that has gained some welcome traction in the marketplace. The second is our work with WAGES. The third is our introduction in 2009 of sustainably harvested palm oil, which is the base ingredient for most of our cleaners. The fourth is our partnership with the Whole Foods, Whole Planet Foundation that is developing micro-enterprise loan programs in Central America.

6.3 Seventh Generation's Global Imperatives

Our next focus was to develop our global imperatives. Global imperatives are designed to be long term. They are the hoped for manifestation of both my own and the company's essence. They represent the world that we dream of, the world as it could be at its best.

These objectives could take 25, 50, even 100 years to achieve, and this is generally not the kind of timeframe within which business is comfortable thinking. That's what makes the pursuit of global imperatives so challenging. They require a complicated mix of many things: a long-term commitment, cooperation with other businesses and organizations, our own ongoing education and development, and the need to look systemically at everything we do.

This is difficult because we live in a world that compartmentalizes almost everything, from business opportunities to environmental problems. None of the issues to which we are committed can be solved with a mind that looks at the world in a deconstructed manner.

Global imperatives also reinforce our belief that the corporation is the most powerful global institution in the world today and that the role of business in society is one of the most important levers for change. They are a key part of our company's work to represent the positive role that business can play. While this proposition must be considered in a systemic light, in the short term our focus is on using our own operations to set an example for other companies to follow and on setting the bar of possibility higher every year.

The development of our global imperatives began with a question: What is Seventh Generation uniquely able to do that the world most needs? Clearly, that's a kind of question that most businesses are not asking. Yet it's one that lies at the heart of our beliefs about the purpose and possibility of business. The likelihood of business having the type of long term, widespread positive impact that this question implies is close to zero unless the process is as intentional as sales and earnings goals.

The question was merely the start of that process, and we began to answer it in 2005 with a first attempt to define our imperatives at our annual all-company retreat held each autumn in Stowe, Vermont.

We'd spent the earlier part of the year creating a working draft of this document, and the imperatives we came up with are scary, inspiring, hopeful, impossible, and awesome all at the same time. But they have changed the way we do business, and we'll never be able to go back. The language we originally employed, however, was overly complex, which made the imperatives hard to remember and even harder to use. You'll find a copy of the original draft in Appendix A. With this in mind, I rewrote them in the spring of 2007. Here is the most recent draft:

Global Imperatives
(Revised 6/7/07)

1. As a Business we are committed to being educators and to encouraging those we educate to create with us a world of equity and justice, health and wellbeing.

2. To achieve this we must create a world of more conscious workers, citizens, and consumers.

3. We are committed to creating a world that is rich in value as contrasted to a world that is rich in artifacts.

4. We will work to create governance and social systems that increase the capacity for understanding differing perspectives and points of view.

5. We believe that our business and all businesses should engage in the personal development of everyone who works for them.

6. We are committed to approaching everything we do from a systems perspective, a perspective that allows us to see the larger whole, not a fragmented, compartmentalized world, not just what we want to see, our own point of view, our own reality, but a world that is endlessly interconnected, in which everything we do affects everything else.

7. We must ensure that, globally, natural resources are used and renewed at a rate that is always below their rate of depletion.

8. And lastly, we are committed to creating a business where all our products' raw materials, byproducts, and the processes by which they are made are not just sustainable but restorative, and enhance the potential of all of life's systems.

The possibilities inherent in these imperatives are the force that gets me up in the morning and into work. They're also why we have such a low turnover rate and have so many people applying for every job opening we have. But they're not for everyone.

Discussion of each of these imperatives is a never-ending process. One of my favorites is number 3: "We are committed to creating a world that is rich in value as contrasted to a world that is rich in artifacts." Sometimes I think that it is our obsession with the accumulation of stuff that lies at the heart of so much of what troubles the world. The belief that faster cars, bigger houses, private planes, and glittering diamonds will fill the void left by the absence of community, relationship, and connection to nature is misguided at best and catastrophic at worst. Yet how often I fall into the very patterns that I hope to change! This is the way of learning to live our imperatives. It is a journey that most likely has no end and will be marked by a gradual progress that celebrates the trip and not the arrival at our destination.

The discussion and rumination that mark our path along the way start with a basic understanding of the imperatives themselves. So let's look at what these global imperatives mean:

"As a Business we are committed to being educators and to encourage those we educate to create with us a world of equity and justice, health and wellbeing."

We need to teach ourselves, our employees, our business partners, the communities in which we do business, and our consumers, how to work together to create a world marked by wellbeing for all, one where we understand that our shared common fate is driven by cooperation and mutual objectives, and is judged by the wellbeing of those that have the least, rather than those that have the most.

"To achieve that we must create a world of more conscious workers, citizens, and consumers."

Consciousness requires intention. It demands that we observe ourselves, and in that observation bring intention and purpose into our thoughts and actions. It means that we must no longer play like a gang of hamsters, each spinning rapidly on his or her own individual wheel, rushing around, following the same pattern over and over again. Instead we must become purposeful individuals who manage our thoughts, words, and actions in ways that create more intentional, selfless, and meaningful effects.

We often get so caught up in what we are "doing" that we lose sight of the effect we seek to have. We get so into cooking that we forget the point of having company over is to celebrate just being together. We create brilliant advertising that everyone notices, though no one can remember the name of the company who created it. We get so focused on pointing out what was wrong with the job someone did, we don't realize that we've left our co-worker so dispirited that they are unlikely to try harder the next time around.

"We are committed to creating a world that is rich in value as contrasted to a world that is rich in artifacts."

We have created a world filled with things that are consuming the resources of the planet faster than they can be regenerated. Most of us are well beyond the point at which all this "stuff" provides happiness and fulfillment. The manufacturing, sale, and accumulation of these artifacts hopelessly promise to replace the richness that's being lost in our increasingly isolated lives, lives which often no longer include the relationships and community that are life's true source of lasting value.

The creation and sale of artifacts is the primary driver of our economy. More artifacts mean more growth. The Australian policy intellectual Clive Hamilton in his 2003 book *Growth Fetish wrote,* "In the face of the fabulous promises of economic growth, at the beginning of the 21st century we are confronted by an awful fact. Despite high and sustained levels of economic growth in the West over a period of 50 years—growth that has seen average real incomes increase several times over—the mass of people are no more satisfied with their lives now than they were then. If growth is intended to give us better lives, and there can be no other purpose, it has failed.... The more we examine the role of growth in modern society, the more our obsession with growth appears to be a fetish—that is, an inanimate object worshipped for its apparent magical powers...."

"We will work to create governance and social systems that increase the capacity for understanding differing perspectives and points of view."

Our system of government has been overrun by businesses imposing priorities that far too narrowly focus our shared resources on their own objectives in order to enrich their management and shareholders. Business must be willing embrace new governance and social systems that ensure the wellbeing, health, justice, and equity of all citizens for generations to come. This will require the willingness to hear and appreciate other voices and points of view.

One essential aspect of understanding differing perspectives and points of view is inviting those with conflicting beliefs to sit at the table with us. Bringing together business, labor, NGOs, religious organizations, and community groups to discuss problems, something known as a multi-stakeholder dialogue, creates possibilities that simply don't exist when we approach issues in a compartmentalized manner.

"We believe that our business and all businesses should engage in the personal development of everyone who works for them."

To fulfill our own possibilities and become all we can be, we must grow ourselves. This is an eternal process, a journey with no destination. It must be nurtured by the business community within which we spend the vast majority of our lives. This development will enable us to bring ever more capabilities to all that we endeavor to do.

"We are committed to approaching everything we do from a systems perspective, a perspective that allows us to see the larger whole, not a fragmented, compartmentalized world, not just what we want to see, our own point of view, our own reality, but a world that is endlessly interconnected, in which everything we do affects everything else."

We live in an increasingly interdependent world of collective destinies and possibilities. As Jeffrey Sachs says, "humanity shares a common fate on a crowded planet." Our future is dependent on global cooperation, trust in people with whom we have only found differences in the past, and a mutual understanding that ultimately we will all sink or swim together. (In Chapter 8, I'll focus more fully on this idea via a discussion of systems thinking.)

"We must ensure that globally, natural resources are used and renewed at a rate that is always below their rate of depletion."

With a global population that has increased by 4 billion in the last 55 years to a total of 6.6 billion souls and economic activity that's increased eight-fold in that same period, humanity is now requiring more resources than the planet can produce or replace. We are rapidly depleting the vital support systems that sustain life on the planet. At our current rate of consumption there will not be adequate fresh water, top-soil, biodiversity, or clean air for the next generation, let alone the next seven generations.

"We are committed to creating a business where all our products' raw materials, byproducts, and the processes by which they are made are not just sustainable but restorative, and enhancing the potential of all of life's systems."

Moving beyond sustainability, we must repair and restore the damage we have done to our planet. We must produce products that are good rather than merely "less bad." Products that don't slow the rate of environmental degradation but instead restore our natural resources. The entire life cycle of the products we sell, or as we call it, the value-adding process, must on a net-basis produce a positive, regenerative effect. This is no small challenge and none of the products we currently sell come close to meeting this standard.

6.4 Walking the Talk: How Seventh Generation is Putting Its Global Imperatives Into Positive Action

To generate solutions to the challenges of our global imperatives, Seventh Generation has created a number of exciting new programs that have both direct and systemic impacts. These include the Change-It program, Tampontification and Show the World What's Inside, our aforementioned partnership with WAGES and the Whole Planet Foundation, our essential oils program, and our sustainable palm oil initiatives. While we hope that everything we do as a company addresses our imperatives in some significant way, these programs were intentionally designed to have the larger impacts to which those imperatives speak.

The Change-It Program

The purpose of Change-It is to train and sustain the next generation of "change agents" by providing comprehensive active education to young people. Change-It works to create a viral movement of regenerative and systemic change that will advance social and environmental justice causes of all kinds.

By recruiting committed student leaders, providing them with exceptional training, enlisting them in systems-changing campaigns, and engaging them through continued support, we believe we can achieve significant environmental and social change.

Founded in 2006, the program is a joint initiative between Greenpeace USA and Seventh Generation. Over the first three years Seventh Generation has invested approximately $1 million in the program, which starts with a week-long training paid for by a scholarship fund created by Seventh Generation. 100 students participated in 2006 and 200 participated in both 2007 and 2008. The program has been a huge success. Eight-five percent of the students that participated in the initial 2006 program committed to staying involved with Greenpeace and Seventh Generation, and more than 40% accepted active positions in the Greenpeace Student Network. These student alumni are now mentoring and training their peers back home to create further ripples of change radiating out from the center we've established.

Ultimately we judge the impact and value of the Change-It program by the activities of the participants following their involvement. There are many stories to tell. A representative example is that of Charlotte Ely, Co-Founder and Board Member of Replant New Orleans (www.replantneworleans.org), a non-profit organization which was founded in October 2006 shortly after the conclusion of the 2006 Change-It program. Replant New Orleans is working on urban reforestation of those areas of New Orleans devastated by Hurricane Katrina.

Charlotte's efforts include a large-scale tree planting along streets and sidewalks, the development of an urban farm, and the creation of a series of large-scale workshops on a variety of subjects, from healthy soil and composting to bio-remediation and sustainable living. Seventh Generation has supported the efforts of Replant New Orleans, which was the focus of Seventh Generation's 2007 Earth Day program. During the month of

April 2007, our One Ton Tree initiative brought together the Seed Collective (www.seedcollective.org) and Replant New Orleans to help restore the urban forest in New Orleans.

Through the Seed Collective's wireless interactive tool (called SEED), anyone could dial a number on their cell phone, plant a virtual seed, and help it grow into a tree on the computer screen using the numbers on their keypad. For each tree grown, Seventh Generation would fund the planting of a real tree in New Orleans by Replant New Orleans.

After the 2008 program, we decided to reflect on our successes and challenges, working towards an upgraded and redesigned program for 2010.

Tampontification

Our Tampontification initiative was another program that supported our global imperatives. Developed in 2005 to introduce a new line of chlorine free sanitary napkins and certified organic tampons, the program used a combination of interrelated issues to inform, educate, and move people to action on two connected but equally taboo subjects: menstruation and homelessness. Because feminine care products are in such short supply in women's shelters around the country, the issue of homelessness was chosen as the focus of the campaign. That campaign lived alongside a discussion of women's periods.

The program had four essential elements: Tampontificate, a blog designed to discuss the taboo subject of menstruation; Donate, an online program that allowed the 700,000 people who visited the site to donate feminine care projects to their local woman's' shelter courtesy of Seventh Generation; Motivate, an online educational effort designed to provide information about the problem of homelessness in the US and encourage people to become involved with homelessness issues and volunteer at their local shelters; and Educate, which provided information about why chlorine- and pesticide-free feminine care products are essential to women's health.

The What's Inside Campaign

In the fall of 2008, Seventh Generation launched the 'Show the World What's Inside' campaign. The campaign focused on the education and promotion of the importance of ingredient disclosure. In conjunction with the campaign launch, Seventh Generation partnered with the Environmental Working Group (EWG) to raise awareness of their DECLARATION initiative and efforts to further passage of the Kid-Safe Chemical Act. In addition, Seventh Generation teamed-up with Dr. Alan Greene in support of his ingredient disclosure campaign. Dr. Greene continues to work with Seventh Generation and speak on behalf of the company on the importance of ingredient disclosure and the relevance to children's health.

In an effort to raise awareness and initiate action on the importance of ingredient disclosure, Seventh Generation launched the 'Show the World What's Inside' campaign on October 11 at the American Academy of Pediatrics National Conference in Boston, Massachusetts. At the event Seventh Generation hosted a panel discussion and press conference to raise awareness on the importance of ingredient disclosure, educate others on the impact conventional cleaner chemicals have on children's health, and show consumers how to take action and learn what's inside the products they use.

6.5 Corporate Direction: The Glue That Holds It All Together

Our corporate direction is designed to provide focus and boundaries to everything the company does as it moves between its essence and its global imperatives. It should not only help us upgrade everything we do, it should also guide our decisions to *not* do something we're not very good at!

Our corporate direction moved though a number of major changes in 2006 and 2007. Currently it states that it is our intention:

To be the authentic force, leading the field of sustainability

At the intersection of human & environmental health
Through personal & home care systems

In a way that consciously co-creates increasing health, hope, and possibility

So that business and individuals actualize their potential to positively impact the world.

This reinforces the idea embodied in our essence that we will be an authentic force in everything we do. That's an important distinction to make: we will be not simply authentic, but an authentic *force*. This implies that we will spread authenticity as we lead the field of sustainability. Our products and product systems must, from all of our customers' many perspectives, impact both human & environmental health in a positive way. That's not something that all our products do today; our paper products, diapers, and feminine care products have no substantiated health benefits.[6]

By defining that we will exclusively focus on personal & home care products, we are committed to not selling food, garden, or automotive products. Note, too, the use of the word "systems," which means that we will work toward "product systems" rather than the individual products we sell today.

What is a product system? The best way to understand this idea is by way of the example of the Apple Computer company. Their entertainment and communication system is totally unique. My MacBook, office computer, iPod, and iPhone all communicate effortlessly with each other. I download music, movies, books-on-tape, podcasts, and TV shows from the iTunes store, which for the most part supplies these things in proprietary formats that can only be played on Apple equipment. This content integrates seamlessly with each of my four devices and allows these different devices to share this content between them on my command. If my iPod breaks, I don't go out and buy whatever MP3 player is on sale. I buy a new iPod because, like a puzzle piece, that's the only product that will fit into the void in my system that's been created. It's the same with each member of my family. Most of us have Apple equipment and have replaced each part of our respective systems numerous times with new Apple gear. We're deeply financially, emotionally, and practically committed to Apple's entertainment and communication system. At this point, it would be both inconceivable and logistically impossible to switch to a different product system.

"In a way that consciously co-creates increasing health, hope, and possibility," means that we will work with each of our key stakeholders, but most importantly our consumers, to create new possibilities for hopefulness and health. Through an interactive dialogue and relationship, we will strive to create this new future together. While this most often might take place through our website, it also includes programs such as Change-It.

Our final statement, *"so that business and individuals actualize their potential to positively impact the world,"* speaks for itself!

Chapter 7
Managing Principles

We've talked a lot in this guide about the things you'll find at Seventh Generation. Here's something you won't find: a document that tells our staff to be honest and nice, that instructs everyone on what to wear to work, that specifies when lunch and breaks are to be taken, and outlines all the others rules of the office. That's because we don't have a lot of rules.

In general we believe that principles are a better guide for the adventure we'll be enjoying together. A principal is a fundamental, primary, or general law or truth from which others are derived. Our principles are one of the most essential factors in our success and one of the key differentiating aspects of our Company.

These managing principles were first developed in early 2008. As our company grew rapidly, I became increasingly concerned about the ability of its senior management to model the ideals that I believed were essential and consistent with our values. If senior managers weren't "being" who we hoped everyone else would "become" our chances for success were slim.

The more we discussed these principles, the clearer it became that they were appropriate expectations for everyone at the company. In essence, they describe the standards to which we will hold ourselves accountable. As with almost everything, they are not absolutes. They don't represent a state of being but rather a process of becoming. They are meant to give voice to an agreed upon goal and to allow for conversation whenever anyone, from myself to you, our newest employee, appears to behave in a manner that's not aligned with their intent.

There are six principles:

1. **Systemic Thinking:** We must be able to demonstrate how we are seeking to be whole and complete in our thinking. This is

essential when launching a major initiative, project, or pursuit. We must be able to present the thinking that underlies a proposal. As described in our global imperatives, "we are committed to approaching everything we do from a systems perspective, a perspective that allows us to see the larger whole, not a fragmented, compartmentalized world, not just what we want to see, our own point of view, our own reality, but a world that is endlessly interconnected, in which everything we do affects everything else.

So how do you know if you're thinking systemically?

The use of frameworks always helps, especially when you're working alone. Picture the working of the thing you're thinking about (i.e., its use), get different perspectives from others', ask yourself what different stakeholders would think. Whenever possible, engage in dialogue with someone else who can observe your own thinking and help you see it more clearly yourself. (System thinking is described in greater detail in Chapter 8.)

2.   **Growth & Development:** Beginning in 2009, everyone must have a Development Plan that shows how we are each growing our own will, being, and function as well as the wills, beings, and functions of those we manage.

Our **Will** is the internal guidance system that generates the passion and desire to do something. It is the opposite of an external system (like a boss or a law) that tells us what we should or must do. We'll always do best at those things we have the most will to do. We can generate our own will toward something. Or others can help us generate will by raising us up and helping us see for ourselves that which is already inside of us.

All our work with others must be realized in a way that builds the will to be increasingly conscious and developmental. This is clearly about going beyond what is traditionally defined as successful.

Being from my perspective is how we are. It is also about what we are helping ourselves to become. In this way, being is both a state of consciousness and intention. Think of it as a question: Am I being the person

I desire to be? The intention of being a particular type of person, or behaving in a certain way is often best achieved by having a specific aim in that direction. For example, I might aim to listen and ask questions, rather than provide answers. Or I might aim to speak my mind, even if I am afraid of what others might think. If I do what I intend to do then I am effectively managing my being.

For its part, **Function** is relatively straightforward. It is about how, and how well, we do what we do. We can function as a teacher, a sales person, an accountant, a mentor, a friend, etc.

As part of our personal growth and development, we must each seek to combine our contributions to personal essence with clarity on those growth opportunities that will generate the greatest value for the company. We must work to be increasingly reflective and conscious, clear about who we seek to become and about the aims that will guide our progress. We must find the courage to take risks without the certainty of knowing where the path we choose will lead. We must use critical thinking in dialogue with others. This kind of reflection along with rigorous examination of our progress and our assumptions will build the courage, flexibility, and capabilities we need to succeed beyond what we imagine possible.

Growth and development requires *taking the chances necessary to become more than we already know how to be.* We must be willing to make a commitment to this idea because it is the ultimate source of the growth and success of our company. Making promises beyond our capabilities means committing to doing something we have never done before and might not even have any idea how to do. It is in risks like this that enormous growth takes place.

We should each be driven by two primary things: internal locus of control and external considerations. Being driven by an internal locus of control means that we are driven by what we believe is right, what we believe the business needs, not waiting for someone else to tell us what to do. Being driven by external considerations means that we keep in mind how what we are doing will affect others, our co-workers, consumers, partners, and our supply chain.

This is scary stuff because it means we are often doing what no one has done before. We get there by being willing to learn how and by a willingness to fail. And we learn how to do it by growing ourselves and others. This means taking risks and being able to clearly articulate both the risks themselves and how taking them will cause us to grow. We simply can't grow or become who we are committed to becoming without risk.

While taking risks is often more than a little unnerving, it yields the greatest rewards.

When Patagonia, for example, decided to use only organic cotton and to institute full closed loop manufacturing, they had no idea how or even if they would succeed, but they made the commitment, and they made it publicly, because they felt it was the right thing to do.

When Greenpeace rated the environmental performance of computer makers, Lenovo was ranked the worst—number 10 out of 10. But the company bravely committed itself to becoming number one in only 18 months. They had no idea how to do this, but they went ahead with the goal anyway because they believed they had to. And they succeeded to the great benefit of their brand; more importantly, to their own confidence in what they were capable of.

And that brings up an important point: Growth also requires the celebration of success. We must be generous in our praise of ourselves and others when we achieve positive growth.

3. **Authenticity, or being who we say we are:** Authenticity to our essence as a company, our global imperatives, and our corporate direction requires that we demonstrate, through the way we manage and work, what it means to be reflective and developmental as leaders. This requires reflection on that leadership. It asks us to proactively look for opportunities to upgrade our process. It requires that we seek out the perspectives of others and become careful listeners. An authentic company can only be led by authentic leaders. As Gandhi said, "We must be the change we seek in the world."

Carol Sanford describes authenticity as a *process capability*—not a state of being. In other words, it is a journey, not a destination. Nothing is totally or completely "authentic." We aspire to always move toward authenticity through transparency, wholeness, and being true to others. We work towards this condition by allowing others to see the whole for themselves, rather than see what we see, believe to be true, want them to see, or believe is important.

Authenticity gives any endeavor its form and determines the state of the ground upon which it grows its potential. Authenticity consists of the following elements, which are experienced by ourselves and all those who are a part of any process. Authenticity exists when:

- *There is Meaning.* This occurs when the quality of our actions and interactions achieves an ability to communicate to one another not just words but the real essence of the object or subject of discussion.

- *There is Wholeness.* Wholeness occurs when we describe a situation, event, or experience to others who were not there and avoid being partial or selective. We strive instead for conveying and discovering the whole of the experience, rather than excluding any portion in order to limit others' ability to develop full meaning and all its implications for themselves. *In wholeness, nothing is withheld.* We speak from the essence of ourselves so that we can represent the same situation in the same way no matter what the audience or situation.

- *There is Receptivity.* This is about taking into account the other person's aspirations and potential. We avoid projecting our own feelings and beliefs onto others and instead consider it part of our responsibility to continually increase our ability to see through their eyes as a way to increase our understanding of each given situation.

4. **Consumer-centricity:** In our every deliberation, we will be guided by our consumers and our consumer buyer classes. They, and only they, keep us in business. Every decision must

be based upon clarity about how what we are choosing to do is aligned with what our consumers want. Our success will only ever be based on how effectively we support and enrich the essence and being of our consumers while still remaining true to our own essence and global imperatives. We must know our consumers by understanding their essence, the sources of their own will, who it is they want to become, and how we can help.

Jeff Bezos, founder of Amazon.com, once recounted a story in the Harvard Business Review about what Amazon does when, while facing a really tough challenge, they get into an infinite loop and can't decide what to do. They find the solution by converting the challenge into a straightforward question: "What's better for the consumer?"

This is a simple but highly effective strategy. And it springs from another realization Bezos had during the company's early days. When Amazon started posting customer reviews, sometimes a customer would trash a book, and the publisher wouldn't like it. Bezos would get letters from publishers saying, "Why do you allow negative reviews on your website? Why don't you just show the positive reviews?" One letter in particular suggested that Bezos and his team didn't understand their business. You make money when you *sell* things, the angry publisher wrote. But Bezos had another more evolved notion, one that lies at the very heart of his company's phenomenal success. Bezos believes that Amazon.com doesn't make money when it sells things; It makes money when it helps customers make buying decisions. And he's absolutely right.

5. **Anticipating the unfolding future.** In the world's rapidly evolving environment, key proposals, decisions, and pursuits must be grounded in an understanding and belief about what the world is "becoming" and how the solution we are championing is grounded in the future we are anticipating.

What looks right today may be dead wrong tomorrow. Just look at the American automobile industry. It failed to "anticipate the unfolding future" of high gas prices, while the Japanese were able to look around the corner and see that success down the proverbial road would be based in large part on energy efficiency, small cars, and high gas mileage.

In our own case, anticipation means that our day-to-day decisions and actions such as hiring, sub-contracting, marketing, and the allocation of resources are not based on simply extending our current known business model into a near future that is based on our past experience but on what is required to build the business we want to be a part of three, five, or even ten years from now.

6.   **Innovation:** In a highly competitive, rapidly changing world, innovation is essential to everything we do. Our products, processes, and services must be driven by a culture deeply committed to innovation. Innovation is rooted in the conscious creation of new patterns.

As we seek to live by these managing principles, *how* we do what we do is as important as what it is we're doing. Every day we must care relentlessly about our coworkers and work to help them conquer their fears and the upset they may feel as they face the multitude of challenges that our business has chosen to take on. We must help lift others up out of their automatic and reactive patterns. We must demonstrate through dialogue and leadership the capability to transform any negative energy into positive will. And we must work to enhance both our individual and collective understanding of how we can better contribute to the effort to become the people we are all committed to becoming.

Carol Sanford describes six axioms regarding the consciousness that is required to do this. These can help all of us attain this important goal:

1. **Pattern Generation:** To be conscious, we must avoid unconscious pattern following and instead demand new pattern generation in our thinking. For the most part, we continually live in and regenerate the same patterns in our lives: the way we respond when annoyed by a spouse or a friend, what we eat for breakfast, whether we're Democrats or Republicans, etc. We often, in effect, live the same life over and over again. Consciousness requires the generation of new patterns, doing what we have never done before, thinking new thoughts, considering new ideas, and being who we want to become in the process.

2. Reflective Intelligence: Reflection, particularly upon our own thinking and thinking processes, helps us to become conscious. Reflection helps us to manage our thinking and behavior *intentionally*.

3. Essence: Our normal "commoditizing and homogenizing" of things, allow us to generalize, categorize, and compartmentalize them and thus prevents us from seeing the essence and uniqueness of any experience.

4. The Examined Life: We become a source of authority when "we" are able to engage deeply in personal and collective examination. This leadership work takes a great deal of effort since we are highly conditioned to accept the word of authorities, experts, and gurus who lie outside ourselves. We must be our own experts and authorities, especially when it comes to who we want to be and what we want to become.

5. Strata of Existence: Consciousness develops as we learn to see that the world does not exist on a single plane or level but rather occupies a strata of perspective and perception. We experience different levels of awareness and sensitivity in ourselves and in others. There is no absolutely "correct" experience—only different points of view and different levels of consciousness. Our level of consciousness when we drive to work is different from our level of consciousness when we decide to go skydiving and prepare to jump for the first time.

7. Locus of Control: We take responsibility for our thoughts and actions and their effects. We avoid the transference of responsibility to others outside of ourselves. We work to see ourselves as the only true cause of our life's outcomes, whether those outcomes are desired or not. We seldom blame others for our failures or disappointments, focusing instead on the role we played in bringing about a result that was less then we had hoped for.

Chapter 8
Thinking Like a System

"We are committed to approaching everything we do from a systems perspective, a perspective that allows us to see the larger whole, not a fragmented, compartmentalized world, not just what we want to see, our own point of view, our own reality, but a world that is endlessly interconnected, in which everything we do affects everything else."
                                    Seventh Generation Global Imperative

Systems thinking is a framework based on the belief that the individual parts of a system can only be understood in the context of the relationships they have with other parts of the system, the system as a whole, and the other systems with which they interact.

Here it's described in excerpts from an article on the subject by Daniel Aronson at the *Thinking Page* (www.thinking.net):

"The approach of systems thinking is fundamentally different from that of traditional forms of analysis. Traditional analysis focuses on separating the individual pieces of what is being studied; in fact, the word 'analysis' actually comes from the root meaning 'to break into constituent parts.' Systems thinking, in contrast, focuses on how the thing being studied interacts with the other constituents of the system—a set of elements that interact to produce behavior—of which it is a part. This means that instead of isolating smaller and smaller parts of the system being studied, systems thinking works by expanding its view to take into account larger and larger numbers of interactions as an issue is being studied. This results in sometimes strikingly different conclusions than those generated by traditional forms of analysis, especially when what is being studied is dynamically complex or has a great deal of feedback from other sources, internal or external.

"The character of systems thinking makes it extremely effective on the most difficult types of problems to solve: those involving complex issues, those that depend a great deal on the past or on the actions of others, and those stemming from ineffective coordination among those involved.

"An example that illustrates the difference between the systems thinking perspective and the perspective taken by traditional forms of analysis is the action taken to reduce crop damage by insects. When an insect is eating a crop, the conventional response is to spray the crop with a pesticide designed to kill that insect. Putting aside the limited effectiveness of some pesticides and the water and soil pollution they can cause, imagine a perfect pesticide that kills all of the insects against which it is used and which has no side effects on air, water, or soil. Is using this pesticide likely to make the farmer or company whose crops are being eaten better off?

"The belief being represented here is that 'as the amount of pesticide applied increases, the number of insects damaging crops decreases.' According to this way of thinking, the more pesticide is applied, the fewer insects there will be damaging crops, and the less total crop damage.

"The temptation is to say that eliminating the insects eating the crops will solve the problem; however that often turns out to not be the case. The problem of crop damage due to insects often does get better—in the short term. Unfortunately, this view represents only part of the picture. What frequently happens is that in following years the problem of crop damage gets worse and worse and the pesticide that formerly seemed so effective does not seem to help anymore.

"This is because the insect that was eating the crops was controlling the population of another insect, either by preying on it or by competing with it. When the pesticide kills the insects that were eating the crops, it eliminates the control that those insects were applying on the population of the other insects. Then the population of the insects that were being controlled explodes and they cause more damage than the insects killed by the pesticide used to.

"In other words, the action intended to solve the problem actually makes it worse because the way its unintended side effects change the system ends up exacerbating the problem. Thus, although the short-term effects of applying the pesticide were exactly what was intended, the long-term effects were quite different.

"With this picture of the system in mind, other actions with better long-term results have been developed, such as Integrated Pest Management, which includes controlling the insect eating the crops by introducing more of its predators into the area. These methods have been proven effective in studies conducted by MIT, the National Academy of Sciences, and others, and they also avoid running the risk of soil and water pollution."

Peter Senge, author of *The Fifth Discipline*, a seminal text on systems thinking, looks at the subject from a business perspective:

"In a systems approach to a problem, you start by realizing that there is no inherent end to a system. There is no such thing as a complete theory. The quest is to look at a problem more comprehensively. The resolutions come from rethinking how we deal with complexity. We all deal quite effectively with many highly complex tasks, like driving our cars.

"How do we do it? We go through a process not unlike what someone goes through to become a concert pianist. Very few people start out playing Mozart. You start out playing something simple, like the scales. At each level we start with a degree of complexity, just within the bounds of our conscious ability or our normal awareness to grasp. Even though our normal awareness only handles a limited degree of complexity, somehow we do learn to deal with incredibly complex tasks.

"Even a great pianist will often begin playing a new piece at a slow tempo. Gradually he picks up the tempo as he 'grasps' the piece as a whole. When the time to perform the piece comes, the pianist no longer requires any 'self-conscious,' waking awareness to concentrate on where his fingers go. He frees that part of his awareness to focus purely on the aesthetic.

"That process is analogous to how we deal with complexity generally. It suggests that parts of our mind deal with complexity much better than our normal, self-conscious, waking awareness. The key to educating people in systems thinking is to use a developmental process— to replicate what the pianist goes through. Eventually the concert pianist can simply look at a piece of music, which to our eyes is hopelessly complex, and absorb it with his self-conscious awareness. He may still have to practice it, but his ability to deal with complexity has expanded. A rapport has developed within his own consciousness between his self-conscious awareness and a more automatic level of consciousness capable of dealing with much greater complexity. Scholars of complex systems have never explained how, out of the hundreds that try and fail, some people are able to masterfully lead complex organizations.[7] We can't explain these successes (other than as blind luck), because we assume the only way people can master systems is through a self-conscious, rational process of analysis and few, if any, executives have the tools to do this.

"In fact, people who succeed in handling complexity are working in an intuitive domain we don't even consider in our educational theories. Only through the integration of that intuitive domain with the normal, rational awareness domain will we transcend mere modeling. In our work with business executives, we start with simple models that are just within the person's ability to grasp. We use these until executives no longer have to think about them very much, and then we step up to more complex models. Simply accepting the complexity is a major step toward developing that intuitive sense. But it is very difficult for business executives to accept that complexity because many of them need to see themselves as being in control. To accept it means they must recognize two things at a gut level: 1) that everything is interconnected, and 2) that they are never going to figure out that interconnectedness.

"One implication of that realization is very liberating, because not only are you never going to figure it out, but neither is anybody else. It creates an inherent equality.

"In the leadership course taught through Innovation Associates, there is an exercise that takes people through a process whereby they discover that they are never going to completely figure anything out in their lives. It has a remarkable impact on people. Some can't quite handle it and try to intellectualize it. But those who can face that simple fact will often sit back in their chairs and laugh, realizing that they are dismantling two common beliefs: first, that people can control an organization from the top or at a distance; and second, that you can ever fully understand a system or figure it out. Dismantling these beliefs is critical to piercing through the hierarchical mentalities that dominate most organizations. Most people have grown up in an authoritarian environment where their parents, teachers, or bosses provided the answers. They are absolutely convinced, deep down, that people above them know what is going on. That mentality weakens them as individuals and weakens the organization as a whole.

"When a group of people collectively recognize that nobody has the answer, it transforms the quality of that organization in a remarkable way. And so we teach executives to live with uncertainty, because no matter how smart or successful you are, a fundamental uncertainty will always be present in your life. That fact creates a philosophic communality between people in an organization, which is usually accompanied by an enthusiasm for experimentation. If you are never going to get the answer, all you can do is experiment. When something goes wrong, it's no longer necessary to blame someone for screwing up—mistakes are simply part of the experiment."

Ours is a highly individualistic culture. In our minds and our mythology, the ideal of the solitary hero facing new frontiers and single-handedly conquering every challenge dominates our self-perceptions as a people. In reality, however, we're the product of one great mass movement after another. We are, in fact, almost totally *inter*dependent rather "independent." So are all of our social and economic systems.

We're also creatures of habit. When things go awry, we think only of those solutions that have worked for us in the past. When this strategy does not work as expected, we tend to do the same thing all over again only more aggressively. But what has failed the first time is almost always destined to fail again, and so things continue to get worse, *because we've failed to understand the system in which we are operating and adjust accordingly.* Specifically, we have failed to understand the interdependencies within the system. This failure creates instabilities in the system for which we tend to blame each other and not ourselves. (Hence the importance of having "an internal locus of control.") These emotional reactions do nothing to fix the original problem or the instabilities created by our inability to solve it. And so a kind of "panic" sets in as we keep trying and failing to make repairs using the same set of solutions, and conditions continually worsen.

Why is this such a common pattern? The answer is simpler than you might think. Regardless of where we might see our "place" in an organization, a family, a community, or a nation, we are part of a human system. Senge points out that the nature of such systems is often a difficult one to perceive *because we are part of the structure.* Just as "the eye can't see the eye," we're usually simply too close to the systems we need to contemplate to easily get a proper perspective.

Players in our systems (and that includes all of us!) look for heroes and, when things go wrong, culprits. We habitually look for someone to blame when instead, we should understand three lessons that Senge offers:

> *1. Structure influences behavior.* "Different people in the same structure tend to produce qualitatively similar results.... More often than we realize, *systems cause their own crises,* not external forces or individuals' mistakes."

> *2. Structure in human systems is subtle.* "Structure in complex living systems (like the human body) means the basic interrelationships that control behavior," including *how* we make decisions and how we "translate perceptions, goals, rules, and norms into actions is often too subtle to be seen."

> *3. Leverage often comes from new ways of thinking.* Our tendency is to focus on our own actions and ignore how they affect others. This creates extreme instability because we don't understand how we are creating the instability in the first place. The answer is to "refine your scope of influence" by being deliberate. From this perspective, increasing consciousness and creating new patterns is critical.

We must work to see and understand the "systemic structure" that Senge says consists of the "underlying patterns of interdependency." The failure to recognize in this way the systems in which we function is what tends to make us feel like "victims."

The interesting thing about the patterns of interdependency is that we tend to be relatively unaware of them. We like to believe the fable of independence despite the inherent fallacy of such mythologies. Senge demonstrates this point with the example of the automobile, which he describes as one of our "prototypical beliefs of independence."

Contrary to the mythical image of freedom with which we endow our cars, we're quite literally placing our lives in the hands of strangers when we drive them. Our roads are "an extraordinarily *inter*dependent system" which we only realize when there is an accident. "We live our lives in webs of interdependence," says Senge. And we must "unlayer" our *mental models* about life, work, and society to navigate these webs.

We learned as children that a consequence usually immediately follows an action. Indeed, this notion is embedded in the Newtonian physics which govern our understanding of the world around us. These natural laws state that every action will produce equal and opposite reaction. Yet sometimes those reactions, those consequences, are not immediately apparent. When this happens, we're confused. And when longer-term consequences are not at all what we expected or wanted, we don't see their connection to our earlier actions.

People consistently take actions that seem to make "good sense" based on the limited information and understanding they have, but they are unable to see the connection to these longer-term consequences. Indeed, many of our problems are the direct result of our "best efforts." As Walt Kelley's immortal comic character Pogo once wisely said, *"We have met the enemy and they is us."*

Senge asks the crucial question, *if we start to think systemically, how might we act differently?* Will systemic thinking make us more able to create what we really want? "The discipline of systems thinking begins with a shift in awareness and consciousness. You become aware of interdependencies," he writes, and you realize that you must function at a pace the system can handle. When we act precipitously, things typically get worse, not better. The action becomes counter-productive. Senge uses the example of a shower with a slow response time. Turn the handle too aggressively and you will freeze then scald alternatively. Haven't we all experienced that?

Senge finds that "the promise of systems thinking is very simple. If we can begin to learn to shift our ways of looking at the world to begin to see the interdependency that actually exists, we will begin to think differently and therefore, we will begin to act differently."

This is a fundamentally important shift to achieve because the condition of working hard and producing outcomes that are not those we want to produce afflicts human civilization worldwide. We have problems all around us and though we know that despite our best efforts these problems persist, we fail to realize that it may be *because* of our "best efforts."

All of this makes systems thinking the most desperately needed discipline in today's complex, often overwhelming, and seemingly out-of-control world. It should be taught in every school and those who've yet to master its application should not be allowed to move out into the world because the world cannot afford to host any more businesses, institutions, religions, or governments that have been designed in the narrow, fragmented manner that has become an unfortunate hallmark of modern civilization.

Our disjointed, linear, cause-and-effect, culprit-focused approaches to dealing with contemporary life and its institutions are not working. "Systems thinking is a discipline for seeing wholes. It's a framework for seeing interrelationships rather than things, for seeing patterns of change rather than static 'snapshots,'" says Senge. He asserts that much of "the unhealthiness" in our world today is directly proportional to our inability to see it as a whole. To correct this, we must develop a keen sense of the "subtle interconnectedness that gives living systems their unique character."

Why do we attempt to solve every problem by breaking it down into unconnected parts and attempting to rebuild each of these pieces independently to re-create a new incomplete whole? Senge says the roots of this approach lie in our culture—in "linear" Western language and the mindset of the Industrial Age.

Senge says there are two kinds of complexity, and that Western people are good at dealing with one but not the other. The first kind of complexity is *detail complexity*. This is a linear, sequential, cause-and-effect, "snapshot" kind of complexity. It's like having all the parts and a clear understanding of how to assemble them into, say, an automobile or a computer. It may be a challenge, but we're very good at this kind of detailed linear complexity where Part A attaches to Part B to create a unit that then attaches to Part C.

The second kind of complexity is *dynamic complexity*. This is more about "process" than product. Its "cause and effect" is subtle at best—and often obscure or totally hidden to us. Its "structures" are the patterns of interrelationships that recur—again and again, but the appropriate interventions are not obvious to us. For these reasons, we're usually not very good at dealing with dynamic complexities. That answer, says Senge, lies in looking for "circles of causality" and understanding the three crucial variables in every system:

1) Reinforcing or amplifying feedback
2) Balancing or stabilizing feedback
3) Delay

Reinforcing feedback is both the engine of growth and the agent of decline. Here momentum is everything regardless of whether it's in a forward/backward or up/down direction. If we think back again to Newtonian physics, we see a partial parallel in the principle that says that an object in motion tends to remain in motion. In the case of reinforcing feedback, we're talking about motion that reinforces itself over time and in doing so increases, or amplifies, its total energy.

Balancing feedback is the force behind all goal-oriented behavior, whether it's acting to accelerate a given movement or put the brakes on it. To continue our Newtonian comparison, an object in motion tends to remain in that same state of motion (speed and direction) until acted on by another force, which in the case of systems thinking is balancing feedback.

Life as we know it is essentially a series of balancing feedback processes. These processes—except for obvious resistance—are difficult to see, so it often looks like nothing is happening when they are at work, whereas reinforcing feedback processes are usually obvious. We can see when things get worse or better but usually have a hard time seeing what's making them that way.

The third factor in circles of causality is *delay*, which simply tells us that balancing feedback can take awhile to affect reinforcing feedback once it's been put into action.

Senge says that we are in a dynamically complex environment "when the effect of one variable on another takes time." But this delay can be troubling because we don't like impediments when we want something done. Patience, after all, is a virtue that is all too absent from modern life.

Yet, failure to recognize systemic delays simply produce "overshoot." This is a situation when we keep acting on situations past the point we should because the effects of our actions cannot yet be seen even though those actions are, in fact, hard at work. What happens then in the system is instability and ultimately a breakdown of one kind or another.

One of the most significant systemic delays in modern times, and one that has produced huge "overshoot," is global warming caused by the effects of CO_2 emissions taking decades to manifest themselves. One could also describe our diets in much the same fashion. I don't immediately gain weight when I eat too much. It often takes many months before I stand on the scale and see that I have overshot the weight I like to maintain.

Senge offers this advice: "Things do happen...*eventually*. The systems viewpoint is generally oriented toward the long-term view. That's why delays and feedback loops are so important. In the short term, you can often ignore them; they're inconsequential. They only come back to haunt you in the long term. Reinforcing feedback, balancing feedback, and delays are all fairly simple. They come into their own as building blocks for the 'systems archetypes'—more elaborate structures that recur in our personal and work lives again and again."

In today's world, business is obsessively focused on short-term results, and we as a society endlessly seek immediate gratification. We have designed our lives in ways that are fundamentally at odds with a systems point of view. Structuring Seventh Generation as a private company was an explicit redesign that has allowed us to counter this dysfunction and deal with the fundamental systemic challenges of our world. Our investment in the development of our community, in advanced product innovation, and the advancement of corporate responsibility in the business community are all driven by the kind of long term perspective that defines systems thinking.

In *The Fifth Discipline*, Senge defines 11 laws of systems thinking.

1. Today's problems come from yesterday's "solutions."
Like global warming or the pesticide that removes the bad bug from the plants but also kills the bees those plants need for pollination, we often simply shift a problem around rather than solve it.

2. The harder you push, the harder the system pushes back.
This is called "compensating feedback." Or as Newton would put it, for every action there is an equal and opposite reaction.

3. Behavior grows better before it grows worse.
Our "solutions" often make things *look* better in the short run but in the long term they are unmasked as no solutions at all. Think nuclear energy.

4. The easy way out usually leads back in.
Familiar solutions, following old patterns, are the easiest to try but are often fundamentally wrong for a given situation.

5. The cure can be worse than the disease.
Our solutions often create more problems than they solve over time because we are not seeing the situation through a systemic lens. The endless and unrestrained use of antibiotics, for example, is creating health issues that are often worse that the ailments that these drugs treat.

6. Faster is slower.
This is the story of the tortoise and the hare.

7. Cause and effect are not closely related in time.
Cause takes time to produce its true effects. And there is a fundamental mismatch between the nature of reality in complex systems and our predominate ways of thinking about that reality.

8. Small changes can produce big results, but the areas of highest leverage are often the least obvious.
It's the difference between our "snapshot" views and the deeper, better understanding achieved through "process" thinking. It's acupuncture as opposed to antibiotics.

9. You *can* have your cake and eat it too—but not at the same time.
Life is not "either-or." Real leverage, obtained through a better understanding of the "circles of causality," can improve both sides of a situation over time.

10. Dividing an elephant in half does not produce two small elephants.
It produces a mess! Living systems have their own integrity. It's OK to see the parts, but we must understand the integrity of the whole.

11. There is no blame.
You and the cause of your problem are part of a single system. The cure lies in your relationship with your 'enemy.'" This is wrapped inside an overarching reality. According to Senge, "there is no outside."

"Everybody shares responsibility for the problems generated by a system," and "the search for a scapegoat (external locus of control) is a blind alley," Senge says. "Nature loves a balance, but many times human decision makers act contrary to the balances and pay the price." The human body requires "homeostasis" to survive, as does any other system, be it an organization or a society. And, says Senge, "That's one of the lessons of balancing loops, with delays. Aggressive action often produces exactly the opposite of what's intended. It produces instability and oscillation instead of moving you more quickly toward your goal."

Portions of this chapter have been adapted from articles appearing in the December 1995–October 1996 issues of The Curious Journal, *the newsletter of Audubon Area Community Services, Inc. in Owensboro, Kentucky (www.audubon-area.com). A compilation of those articles, which serves as a useful summary of Senge's theories and work, can be found at www.audubon-area.com/sengesum.pdf.*

Chapter 9
You Can't Grow a Business Without Growing People

2,500 years ago, citizens in the city of Athens practiced a form of participatory democracy that provided constant opportunities for personal growth by allowing each person to partake in every aspect of the city's governance. The Athenian democracy created shared responsibility and the experience of a collective journey. In their book, *A Company of Citizens*, authors Brook Manville and Josiah Ober present a roadmap for business based in part on this system. One review of the book noted:

> "Membership in the city's leadership was rotated among all citizens. Everyone's voice was welcome. The citizens and their community lived by a code that Manville and Ober describe as 'moral reciprocity' which 'provided the essential link between 'What's in it for me?' and 'What's in it for us?,' eliminating the conflict between self-interest and community interest. Manville and Ober contrast the open, inclusive environment of ancient Athens with the 'closed doors of executive offices and conference rooms,' where decisions are made by a small group of 'insular elites.' Indeed, 'the entire shape of the modern company reflects a fundamental distrust of its members,' the authors argue."

The society that resulted from this grand experiment attracted the world's best talent. Philosophers, scientists, poets, and artists throughout the Mediterranean flocked to Athens to be part of this new cultural experience. "Citizens had both the right and the obligation to play an active role in the society's governance. At some point in their lives most of Athens 30,000 citizens had the opportunity to participate as a leader." This, in many respects, is what we are trying to recreate at Seventh Generation.

Though business talks endlessly about how human resources are its most valuable asset, most who work in corporate America would be hard pressed to find much evidence to back up this self-professed belief. There is, however, plenty of evidence to suggest that employees in general feel they are among the least appreciated resources a company might have.

A fairly stunning March 7, 2004 Gallup poll, for example, revealed that only 26% of U.S. employees are fully engaged with their job at any one time, and 19% of employees are actively disengaged. The annual nation-wide cost to employ this actively disengaged group exceeds $300 billion. Such findings send a clear message that if a business wants to grow in a sustained and sustainable manner, it must also "grow" the people it employs. It cannot simply train or teach employees but must instead develop them as whole people. It must recognize that full potential only comes through engaging the whole person—body, mind, and spirit.

9.1 Wandering Into Waldorf

When we moved to Vermont in 1995, my wife was committed to providing our children with the private school education that she never had. Unfortunately there weren't many options. We settled on the Lake Champlain Waldorf School in Shelburne. The school building was painted with pastel colors and the rooms were designed in any shape but square. We knew nothing about the Waldorf educational experience and were mildly uncomfortable with what felt like a dated 60s orientation that insisted on wooden toys; no movies, TV or computers; German language instruction; the celebration of holidays we had never heard of (like Michaelmas and Martinmas); and what seemed to be an odd overabundance of fairies and gnomes. Our children would learn how to knit, make wooden eggs, and play two instruments. We worried about whether or not they would learn enough to be ready for college when the time came. Little did I know that I had stumbled upon an educational philosophy that would mirror the educational elements I would come to believe are essential for our own staff.

Waldorf education was developed by a man named Rudolf Steiner, who sought to create a schooling system that would not only facilitate the inclusive, balanced development of children, but would also act in a socially responsible and transformative fashion. At the time, that was a fairly audacious goal. The road to achieving it, however, began in an extremely inauspicious place.

In April of 1919, Rudolf Steiner visited the Waldorf Astoria cigarette factory in Stuttgart, Germany. The German nation had recently been defeated in war and was teetering on the brink of economic, social, and political chaos. Steiner spoke to the workers about the need for social renewal and a new way of organizing society and its political and cultural life. Emil Molt, the owner of the factory, was impressed and asked Steiner if he would agree to establish and lead a school for the children of the employees of the company. Steiner consented but set four conditions, each of which went against the common practice of the day:

One, that the school be open to all children; two, that it be coeducational; three, that it be a unified twelve-year school; and four, that the teachers would have primary control of the school with minimum interference from outside. Steiner's conditions were radical, but Molt gladly agreed to them, and on September 7, 1919, the independent Die Freie Waldorf-schule (Free Waldorf School) opened its doors. Steiner's philosophy and methods proved enduring. Today there are more than 800 Waldorf schools in over 40 countries.

A survey of Waldorf school graduates shows that they share four predominant traits: They keenly value the opportunity to think for themselves and to translate their new ideas into practice. They appreciate and practice life-long learning. They value lasting human relationships and seek out opportunities to be of help to other people. And they are uniquely guided by an inner moral compass that helps them navigate the trials and challenges of their professional and private lives, into which they carry high ethical principles.

Professors who have taught Waldorf students as college undergraduates notice something else: Most have a holistic thinking style, which often includes the ability to "think outside the box," and the ability to integrate seemingly unrelated subjects with clarity and courage.

Another thing Waldorf students seem to share is a capacity for creativity and imagination. Waldorf's emphasis on the visual arts seems to have endowed its students with an ability to see more than others and given them more confidence in the power of their imagination.

Waldorf students also tend to have different priorities than much of the world. When asked to rank which aspects of their current or most recent employment were most important to them, Waldorf graduates rated "good work atmosphere," as very important or extremely important, followed by "ethical principles of the profession," "chance to help others," "chance to introduce one's own ideas," and "self-reliance at work." By contrast very few graduates rated "high income," or "life-long job security" as very or extremely important.

Waldorf schools have flourished in some of the most polarized communities on the planet. Under the apartheid regime in South Africa, a Waldorf school was one of the few in which children of both races attended the same classes. The Waldorf training college in Cape Town, was described by UNESCO as an organization that had a great influence on the conquest of apartheid.

In Israel, the Harduf Kibbutz Waldorf School includes both Jewish and Arab faculty and students, and provides Arab-language Waldorf teacher training. In Brazil, Waldorf teacher Ute Craemer founded a community service organization that provides training and work, health care, and Waldorf education in the poverty-stricken slums of the city of Favelas.

When we enrolled our children in the Lake Champlain Waldorf school, my wife and I knew none of this. And we watched in amazement as what felt to us like a second set of parents helped our three children grow into increasingly extraordinary young people. It was only twelve years later that I made the connection between Rudolf Steiner's vision and what we were trying to create at Seventh Generation.

9.2 Carol Sanford Revisited

We've discussed our work with the consultant Carol Sanford in previous chapters and now it's time to return to it again. Carol, as you may remember was hired in the summer of 2005 to help us develop a strategic plan. She was the first person I ever heard say that, "you can't grow a business without growing the people who are working there." She went so far as to say that personal development was one of the most effective tools available to businesses for generating exponential sales, profits, and shareholder value.

Carol said she helped, "businesses and organizations build the capability to strategically position themselves for non-displace-ability in their markets; build developmental leaders that grow people as they execute strategy; and redesign structures, systems, and processes of the operation to embed strategically focused regenerative practices into daily work.

Sounds intriguing. But what the hell does that mean?

Carol's website provides some insights:

"The most important factor in innovation, growth and business success is something no one talks about directly. It is something everyone can feel, but not everyone can name. It is the human consciousness factor.

"Human consciousness is the ability to exercise the capacities that make us fully human. Are we bringing a way of thinking and acting that makes us creative, flexible as well as disciplined in our strategic thinking and execution? In our development of people? In our work change processes? Only with seeing HOW we are thinking and by managing ourselves can we continuously raise the bar on what is possible. Without consciousness we repeat patterns when new ones are demanded, go down side roads leading away from the future to which we aspire, and choose partial solutions and approaches because we cannot manage which 'mind' we use when we set ourselves to thinking as executive teams. We satisfy ourselves with 'thoughting,' not thinking, bringing old thoughts and ideas into the present conversation and not even noticing. It is a fundamental executive task to know you can develop and manage consciousness, and how to awaken the human consciousness factor, the underlying principle for growing businesses, people and nations."

With that in mind, Carol's aim was to help us create what she called a developmental organization, one "in which every employee is a source of creativity and in which all employees are self-organizing and working together to create a self-organizing business." To create this developmental culture she would help us build a systemic set of 4 interwoven capabilities, each of which nourishes the development of the others.

These are described in her book *The New Paradigm in Business*:

"Self-Reflection—Being able to see, in any situation and at any point in time, the patterns that dominate my thinking and interactions, and to understand their source. This is the essential first step toward the development of self-accountability.

"Regenerative Systems Thinking—Being able to hold in my mind, while engaged in my day-to-day activities, a picture of myself as one of a series of dynamic, evolving systems. Each of these systems is continuously engaged, directly or indirectly, in a multitude of complex interactions and associations. Thus, I see myself as part of a team whose performance and well being I impact and am impacted by. My team impacts and is impacted by the business unit it is part of, which, in turn, is within the corporation and so on out in ever widening spheres of influence. Within this context, I can understand and appreciate the implications and significance of my patterns of thinking and interacting and, through that, take a second step toward self-accountability.

"Integration of Personal Development and Performance Improvement—Being able to utilize every effort to improve the business' performance as an opportunity to develop myself, and every opportunity to develop myself as an opportunity to improve the businesses performance.

"Holographic Approach to Work—Being able to bring to every decision-making process a total perspective that holds within it a reflection of all the critical elements which make up the whole of the business."

After my first meeting with Carol, I wrote her a note to more specifically define what we hoped to achieve as a result of the process. I painted a picture of the company I hoped we would become:

We have a clear sense of purpose, understand who we are and what we are not. We are able to know individually and collectively when we are on and when we are off "the path."

We can make decisions and set priorities out of a "knowing" what we are committed to achieve. Those decisions make sense to the whole community because they have a shared sense of purpose and "knowing."

We relate to each other in a manner that is consistent with our values. All conversations are "real conversations." We tell each other all that there is to/needs to be told—rather than engage in triangulated conversations.

We are seen as an/the absolute leader in conducting business in a new paradigm that unifies the needs of all stakeholders (employees, investors, the planet, etc.) This leadership is one we share with others as a teacher & guide. This leadership is driven by our authenticity, transparency, openness, and exceptional financial results.

Customers who engage with us, initially by buying our products, and ultimately joining our community and becoming advocates/evangelists for our "cause" experience the relationship as one that helps them "let their soul shine."

Our brand is an icon for redefining the relationship consumers have with the stuff they buy. As brands like Patagonia & Working Assets have achieved, the relationship with the brand is based on an alignment of values, and a sense of partnership in a common journey.

We are able to remain an independent company by controlling our ownership. We are able to provide exceptional financial benefits to our employees that afford them financial security.

Anyone who enters our office or speaks with someone on our staff experiences the "extraordinary."

A core part of our business becomes education. Beyond educating stakeholders through the products we sell, we create a highly profitable business model that engages in direct education that leads to greater products sales based on a new awareness and understanding of heath & environmental issues.

We have the financial resources to address the systemic issues that make things "unhealthy"—because "externalities" are not included in the cost we pay for the products and services we purchase, unsustainable products are artificially cheap and sustainable products are artificially expensive. We must change the underlying metrics of our economy to a system of "full cost accounting" so consumers make choices that are in the long term best interest of our society.

To achieve our objectives, we created a "Change Leadership Team" (CLT) consisting of 12 senior and middle managers and two staff members, and embarked on a journey of discovery.

We immediately faced several challenges. How do we keep the whole company aligned with our process and spread to the whole community all we were learning in our monthly two-day sessions with Carol? And how do we spare that much time to begin with? Given the company's unrestrained growth, devoting two days a month to the process was a huge commitment that created a fair amount of stress as emails went unanswered and work went undone.

People also learned at vastly different rates, which often left some confused and frustrated. There was, too, the issue of relevance. While much of what we learned was fascinating, it often seemed hard to connect to our business. It was difficult enough to simply remember two days of intensive learning let alone integrate it into our work. And it wasn't always clear what our new insights had to do with our business.

The process was designed to have three phases: Phase I would establish our strategic direction. Phase II would develop the leadership needed to ensure that the company moved in an aligned fashion and achieved results. Phase III would "operationalize" the strategy and include a redesign of all of our systems and processes.

We launched the process at our annual all-company retreat at the Trapp Family Lodge in Stowe, Vermont. That retreat had a very focused purpose: to build the increased collaborative capabilities needed to run our business with the kind of consciousness that would ensure our ability to live up to the highest intentions of the Core Purpose of Seventh Generation.

One of the first things the CLT had learned was how to write what Carol called "task cycles." These were brief statements that defined the purpose, process, products, and new capability that would result from any significant meeting or project. Task cycles caught on quickly throughout the company and proved to be an invaluable tool. Thinking them through in advance of a meeting, usually made that meeting much more effective, and shorter too!

After the retreat we asked everyone to answer three questions. The group's individual answers showed a surprising consensus and can be summarized as follows:

What do you want to embed in your everyday work?
Take spirit and process to guide us in a way that will help us grow the business and grow personally.

What changed for you?
A newfound respect for others in community, their ideas, and what they offer the whole.

What do you hope for and to what do you aspire?
To be a solution rather than an issue or problem, a contributor to the whole, and stay connected to the process.

9.3 The Difference New Perspectives Make

As of this writing, I've spent nearly 20 years of my life at Seventh Generation, the first twelve of which were devoted to simply trying to ensure that a business that rarely made money somehow survived. At the time of our work with Carol, it was fair to say that I was somewhat, if not totally, burned out. I was unclear whether I had the passion and capability to lead the company into the future.

Perhaps the single greatest benefit of the process that Carol led us through was that I reacquired my own passion for what Seventh Generation was doing and rediscovered how I could contribute to its success. I was able to say for the first time that this was what I wanted to spend the rest of my life doing.[8]

Much of my personal revelation was related to the work Carol did to help me clarify both my "essence" and the "essence" of the company. To see my essence I needed to reflect on the themes that emerged repeatedly throughout my life. What did they tell me about the "process" I used, the "values" that were most important to me, and ultimately the "purpose" that seemed to drive most of what I did. (We talked about this in more detail in Chapter 6.)

Achieving this newfound clarity about my essence and purpose was like a fog lifting to reveal a perfect sunrise over the ocean. It was amazingly energizing, and it provided me with a new sense of my own mission in life. Though it wasn't immediately clear how my self-discovery related to my work, over time I was able to bring the two together and renew my passion for my work in the process.

9.4 Putting It All To Work

While our time with Carol produced all kinds of new thinking, it would be a full two years until I would begin to truly understand the transformative power of some of the ideas we were learning. It also took me awhile to realize that these ideas required more intentional focus on my own growth than I had ever experienced.

On a perfect late summer Wednesday in 2007, just before the Labor Day weekend, I sat with about 35 members of our staff in an all-day voluntary "personal development" session. By mid afternoon I was working with several co-workers on a self-selected personal development problem. I had chosen the long-term struggle I experienced as I tried to move out of the day-to-day operations of the business. To organize our thinking, we used what Carol calls frameworks, multi-dimensional structures that push us to see what often remains out of sight due to our tendency to look at the world through habitual patterns that cause us to see the same things over and over. Patterns are "neural highways" that channel our thoughts. Every time we follow such a pre-established road, we end up making it a little wider and more solid, which makes it that much less likely that we'll go off in a different direction.

These highways and the patterns they represent are like the Colorado River flowing through the Grand Canyon. The longer it flows, the deeper it gets. Every time you ride a raft down the river you see the canyon from the same perspective and it looks mostly the same. But if we decide to walk along a ridgeline instead, we might think we are in a whole different part of the world. The same canyon looks entirely different, as does the sky, the geology, and the river itself. We see things we have never seen before.

Frameworks are like walking on the canyon's rim after spending a lifetime floating through its bottom. They lift us out of old patterns and allow us to see what we have not seen before in an intentional, structured manner. They increase our consciousness and allow us to find new possibilities. They help us grow and develop.

The particular framework we were using that Wednesday afternoon is called the "Law of Three." This is a conflict resolution framework that facilitates a solution that's not about one person acquiescing to another or compromises that leave one or both parties in a state of unhappiness. It's not even about reaching a consensus. The Law of Three is a way for two people (or two groups of people or even a single person talking to themselves) to reach reconciliation.

Reconciliation is defined as "the ending of conflict or renewing of a friendly relationship between disputing people or groups; the making of two or more apparently conflicting things consistent or compatible." It's about finding a solution that lifts up the possibilities for both parties through a process of discovering something that was outside of what either person had considered.

In this situation, my team was helping me think about my process of moving out of the day-to-day management of Seventh Generation. This was something that had been my priority for several years. I'd made some progress but never enough to allow me time to pursue those passions that lay outside the business. I believed that the ultimate solution was to name someone else as President of the company, but with the company growing at 40% a year, my involvement was going to be very difficult to reduce.

As we talked (dialogue is an essential part of the process), we explored the other constraints to reducing my involvement: my frequent message that anyone at the company could come and talk to me at any time; my perpetual instinct to always want to make everything OK and my propensity to always rush into anything that looks like a crisis in order to try and fix it. My willingness to read any email that anyone in the company sent me as well as those from thousands of people I didn't know; and my willingness to attend any meeting to which I'm invited. I quickly began to see that the biggest single restraint that I faced in trying to reduce my day-to-day role might, in fact, be me. It was likely myself that had to change not a set of external factors that I had much less control over. I needed to grow me in order to continue to grow the company.

That was the kind of experience that many of us had that day, and it's not one that most people expect to have at work. We were working at building the greater consciousness essential to growth.

Over the course of the first two years we worked with Carol, we generated a lot of frustration, confusion, and conflict. But we also created a huge amount of new capability, growth, and development. I watched as individuals that I'd often previously avoided contact with because they were so closed and defensive grew into open, self-reflective leaders. I saw one of our smartest senior managers, someone who always had "the answer" but had a very hard time listening to anyone else, develop into a leader who led by helping others discover their own answers.

There were other beneficial outcomes to our work with Carol as well. The Change-It program with Greenpeace was created to replace a simplistic and far less joyful promotion to give away laundry machines. The company's turnover rate, which was already low, dropped to almost zero. Sales per employee rose from slightly more than one million dollars to almost one and a half million. Meetings were shorter, more focused, and productive.

Three years into the process of becoming a "developmental" company we've experienced another startling outcome. In 2006, 2007, and 2008 we had the three most successful years in the company's history. In 2008 alone, sales growth was 50%. Something is working even if we can't always figure out what it is!

What's clear is that we've come a long way but still have miles to go before we sleep and achieve most of what we set out to do. Not everyone has enjoyed the journey, and not everyone supports the investment we've made in the process. Even ardent believers like myself have struggled at times to justify the time and money we've spent. In many respects, we keep discovering that the more we learn the further we have to go, an ongoing realization that continually pushes whatever vague finish line might exist farther into the distance. Yet in all this, for myself at least, a basic truth remains: this process is the path most likely to lead to the fulfillment of our essence and global imperatives. And for that there is no burden too great to bear.

Chapter 10
The Journey of a
Developmental Leader

"The physical survival of the human race depends on a radical change in the human heart...(S)mall changes at just the right place can have a systemwide impact because these changes share the unbroken wholeness that unites the entire system.

"(T)rue leadership is about creating a domain in which we continually learn and become more capable of participating in our unfolding future. A true leader thus sets the stage on which predictable miracles, synchronistic in nature, can—and do—occur. (T)he deeper territory of leadership—collectively 'listening' to what is wanting to emerge in the world, and then having the courage to do what is required."

Joseph Jaworski in *Synchronicity*

I aspire to be what Jim Collins describes as a "Level 5" leader, someone with a combination of "deep personal humility and intense professional will." This involves no small amount of personal growth, and sometimes I forget that my job, or the job of any leader for that matter (and all of us at Seventh Generation are leaders), is more about growing myself than growing others. It is, or at least seems to be, easier to nurture others than myself. I usually have a point of view about who everyone else needs to be or become to do their jobs better while such clarity about myself is often elusive.

For me, leading a business is like sailing. At times, I notice that the hand I've placed on the tiller of the boat trembles, and that that trembling produces vibrations in the boat that slow it down. I notice that I am inclined to change directions when it seems that we are not sailing quick enough. These actions may seem impulsive or reactive. But never having sailed across this part of the ocean, I can't know how fast we're going relative to our potential and whether our heading will get us to our destination when we need to arrive.

There are times, many of them in fact, when the tiller is best left to someone else. That doesn't mean I don't want to be on the boat, or even chart its course, only that holding the tiller takes a steady and experienced hand.

I often tell my team, "When you see the me I need to become before I do, when you see the need for someone else to hold the tiller, don't be afraid to tell me. It takes many people to guide the voyage of a large vessel. I want to always find the place on the boat where I can create the greatest value on and for the trip. That place will always be different for each of us.

It is only through you being the person you aspire to be that you can help me become the person I aspire to be. We are mutually dependent, inextricably bound together on the journey to honor our opportunity, fulfill our possibility, and be the generation that leaves the world in a better state than it was left to us.

Being at Seventh Generation is a commitment to being a leader. And being a leader at Seventh Generation is a commitment to serve as a resource to others in their own leadership journey. This means enabling others to become all they can be and to helping them become passionate about their growth in a way that accelerates your own. Resourcing others is an essential part of the developmental culture we are creating.

To become a leader, someone committed to the endless evolution, development, growth, and recreation of one's self, requires great teachers. I have been fortunate to have many. Some, like Carol Sanford, C. Otto Scharmer, and Peter M. Senge, we've discussed. Others appeared in my life's earlier chapters and live on inside me, people like Wilson Alling, David Sundaram, Marshall McLuhan, and R.D. Lang.

Below is an extended excerpt from a paper written in 2001 by C. Otto Scharmer, W. Brian Arthur, Jonathan Day, Joseph Jaworski, Michael Jung, Ikujiro Nonaka, and Peter M. Senge entitled *Illuminating the Blind Spot: Leadership in the Context of Emerging Worlds*. The paper reflects upon the results of a global project that interviewed 25 leading thinkers on knowledge and leadership. (The full text of all the interviews, as well as an executive summary, is available at www.dialogonleadership.org)

The Blind Spot articulates how the changing nature of the world around us requires changes in the way we manage.

10.1 The Challenge

We Live, Lead, and Work in an Era of Clashing Forces

The waves of change sweeping the world—digitization, globalization, demographic shifts, migration, and individualization, as well as the rapid degradation of social and natural capital—are giving rise to arenas of clashing forces. These clashing forces play out as tensions between multiple polarities: speed and sustainability, exploration and exploitation, global and local ways of organizing, top-down and bottom-up approaches to leadership.

Although general statements like the one above have been true at many times and places in human history, there is something different about today's circumstances. The pace of change is somehow faster, the frequency and amplitude of restructuring and reforming are significantly greater, and the pathways of emerging futures seem to be less predictable than they were in earlier times.

The New Leadership Challenge Is to Sense and Actualize Emerging Opportunities

As the economic foundations of our business world are transformed from more stable patterns to more dynamic patterns characterized by the "forming, configuring, locking in, and decaying of structures," the nature of leadership changes too. In this new environment, real power comes from recognizing the patterns of change. In environments where small differences can cause powerful effects the task of a leader is to sense and recognize emerging patterns and to position him—or herself, personally and organizationally, as part of a larger generative force that will reshape the world. In order to do well in an economy driven by high technology and innovation, business leaders will have to develop and deploy the capacity to sense and seize emerging business opportunities.

For Leaders, What Is "Real" Has Changed

In traditional and more stable business environments, mental-social and generative processes were considered peripheral "complications" in a value chain largely based on the primacy of the physical world. In today's more organic and dynamic business environments, "value constellations" are largely based on intangible resources and the primacy of web-shaped patterns of relationships. The intangible dimension—that is, the generative domain of human action and relationships—is moving from the periphery to center stage. This shift becomes evident when one understands the informal social networks essential to all work, the role of mental models, and the emerging patterns of interdependence among complex and highly distributed (or dispersed) processes of innovation. Accordingly, measures that used to account for the hard variables are increasingly seen as abstract and secondary, while soft variables such as intentions, interpretations, and relationships are increasingly considered part of the more concrete and primary sphere of value creation. Hence, the core of what is considered real has moved from the more tangible to the more intangible variables of social behavior and managerial action. What follows from this for management is that leaders, in order to do well, will have to learn to pay attention to a different set of variables: the variables that used to be referred to as "soft," such as intentions, interpretations, and identity.

Plus Ça Change, Plus C'est La Même Chose

And yet, in spite of all the talk about the new economy—and the new leadership its nonlinearity supposedly requires—actual leadership behaviors often are unchanged: "plus ça change, plus c'est la même chose"—the more things change, the more they stay the same. Wanda Orlikowski of MIT has said that people seem to be "doing more of the same. Very often, even though the espoused goal is to change the way we work with new technology, in reality our practice is often to do more of the same. The technology changes. How we work doesn't. It's rare to find people really doing things differently, improvising, innovating, and changing the work structures that they operate within."

While the world is becoming more interconnected through technology, people's lives seem to become more disconnected. Lucy Suchman of Xerox PARC and Lancaster University suggests that we are increasingly preoccupied with self-referential worlds that leave us isolated and disconnected from what is going on in the world around us. Or as Andy Grove of Intel has put it: "This business about speed has its limits. Brains don't speed up. The exchange of ideas does not really speed up, only the overhead; that slows down the exchange. When it comes down to the bulk of knowledge work, the 21st century works the same as the 20th century." In spite of the apparent need for new ways of leading, strategizing, and organizing, real management processes—in most organizations and companies—have changed very little. Thus, the challenge for leaders is to develop the "knowledge for action" (Chris Argyris) that helps them achieve the essence of post-industrial leadership: to develop higher qualities of pattern recognition and innovation by shifting the place from where a system operates—that is, by becoming more mindful of the deep sources from which behavior and profound innovation and change emanate.

10.2 An Overarching Theory

Experience Must Inform Strategy and Leadership

We believe that an important blind spot in 20th-century philosophy, social science, and management science lies in *not seeing the full process of social reality formation*. In everyday experience we do not see what precedes managerial action and entrepreneurial action—the thought processes that gradually lead to the development of entrepreneurial ideas and initiatives. We do not see the full process of coming-into-being of social action, we do not see its descending movement from thought and consciousness to language, behavior, and action. We see *what* we do. We also form theories about *how* we do things. But we are usually unaware of the *place* from which we operate when we act. Says Master Huai-Chin Nan, a noted Chinese Taoist-Buddhist-Confucian scholar and teacher: "What has been lacking in the 20th century is a central cultural [unifying] thought....We have not gotten into the center: What is human nature? Where does life come from? What is life for? Where does consciousness come from? No one can answer those questions today."

Implications

The Most Important Tool for Leading 21ˢᵗ-Century Change Is the Leader's Self

An effective leader will have the capacity to use his or her Self as the vehicle—the blank canvas—for sensing, tuning in to, and bringing into presence that which wants to emerge. William O'Brien, the former CEO of the Hanover Insurance Company, has summarized his experiences in leading change as follows: "The success of an intervention depends on the interior condition of the intervenor." In other words, the success of a tangible move in a particular situation depends on the Self of the intervenor.

As we wake up and start another day as business leaders, what does this mean to us? How do we remember all this great theory and advice? How in the midst of the next crisis, stressful budget meeting, painful personnel issue, or conflict with a fellow staff member does anyone remember any of this?

The answer is that in many cases we won't. And it doesn't really matter. What matters instead are those few times in between when we successfully stop ourselves from repeating the same pattern and find that sliver of intention, extra awareness, and self-consciousness needed to create a different pattern and a new possibility.

Seven personal practices have helped me establish the admittedly limited awareness process that I have. They sound simple, but I find that they are elusive and hard to practice consistently:

1.   **Stay healthy mentally and physically.** Exercise and don't schedule too many meetings or too much travel. Leave 25% of my time open and unstructured—to read, wander the office, take a walk outside, have an unplanned conversation, enjoy a quiet lunch and observe what's happening around me. If I don't do this I am unlikely to generate new patterns.

2.   **Make sure that I have someone at work who is my resource** in the process, someone who can question me about a decision I

made or am about to make, who observes me in meetings, challenges my behavior, and questions me about how I'm spending my time.

3. **Stop and reflect.** At the end of every meeting, stop and ask everyone to reflect on the experience. How did the meeting go for them? Were they who they wanted to be? Did the meeting fulfill its purpose? Did it have the effect they'd hoped it would? It's about asking questions but not providing answers, being relentlessly honest, and reflecting without reacting.

4. **Always have an "aim."** To become who you want to become it always helps to have a very specific goal, one that you can tell in a moment if you're fulfilling. Usually it helps to have an aim that you believe will create the most value for you and the business, but any aim is better than none. I've had a lot of goals over the course of my life, and often I have returned to those I thought I had mastered in order to master them again or master them better. Examples of these aims include "ask more questions and provide less answers," "reflect don't react," or "create focus."

5. **Rate your own progress.** At the end of the day, I stop for a few minutes to review how the day went. Was I the person I want to become? Did I fulfill my aim, not take the phone call I decided I wouldn't take, not have the meeting that was focused on things that aren't essential, etc.?

6. **Celebrate the journey.** There is no finish line. The process of growth and development is never-ending.

7. **It's what you don't know that counts.** We all know little of what there is to learn and the unimagined possibilities are always far greater and more numerous than those we put in our business plans. I strive to enjoy the humility of not knowing

and to understand that in this perennial state of unknowing I will never be alone.

Peter Senge has defined this process from a different perspective:

"For me the fundamentals (required of a leader) start with a set of deep capacities with which few in leadership positions today could claim to have developed: systems intelligence, building partnership across boundaries, and openness of mind, heart, and will. To develop such capacities requires a lifelong commitment to grow as a human being in ways not well understood in contemporary culture. Yet, in other ways, these are the foundations for leadership that have been understood for a very long time. Unfortunately, this ancient knowledge has been largely lost in the modern era."

Leadership is an art ultimately measured by the success of those we lead. At Seventh Generation we are just now learning how to create leaders. We are blessed with much natural talent but still figuring out how that talent can best be deployed as a resource that will cultivate others. As with everything we do, this also is a journey with no end or final destination.

Chapter 11
Radical Transparency

One morning in mid-March of 2008, I awoke to headlines you hope live only in a bad dream.

Seventh Generation Battles Carcinogenic Chemical Controversy

*'Organic' and 'Natural' Consumer Products Found
Contaminated with Cancer Causing Chemical*

The Organic Consumers Association, a public interest non-profit organization, had released a report showing that 47 organic and natural consumer products contained detectable levels of a contaminant called 1,4-dioxane. Seventh Generation's dish liquid was one of the brands named in the study. This revelation challenged our honesty and transparency and thereby threatened one of our most valuable assets: our reputation.

Of course, we were not intentionally adding 1,4-dioxane to our dish liquid. As the *Los Angeles Times* noted, the compound is a byproduct of a process used to improve the degreasing agent in detergents. Our manufacturers vacuum strip the 1,4-dioxane found in our own products to minute levels, and the OCA report showed that our dish liquid had the least amounts of 1,4-dioxane of all the dish liquids tested. In fact, our levels were fifty times lower than another so-called "natural" brand. That said, we did not argue with the OCA's core assertion and agreed that 1,4-dioxane doesn't belong in our products. The contaminant is simply unacceptable and its presence in our products is contrary to who we are and what we stand for.

But it was not something of which we were unaware or ignoring. Indeed, we'd spent the prior six years working hard to remove 1,4-dioxane from both our dish and laundry detergents, and it was sad to see our incomplete progress characterized as a dishonest act.

But the truth is that our effort was simply not good enough. Not because we haven't yet succeeded in getting rid of 1,4-dioxane[9] but because we excluded consumers and key stakeholders from our conversations about this issue. The problem wasn't highlighted on our web site or detailed in our earlier corporate responsibility report. In this we failed.

And therein lies the larger lesson about what it takes to be a transparent company. We had had hundreds of meetings and conversations about how to purge 1,4-dioxane from our products. We ran many of our own tests and worked closely with raw-materials suppliers and manufacturers. But we didn't take the one most essential step: to share our trials and tribulations with everyone who wanted to weigh in, express their concerns, ask their questions, and challenge our progress (or lack thereof).

Five or six years ago, the expectations around transparency were somewhat more relaxed than they are today. I suppose a part of me hoped that by the time 1,4-dioxane became a public issue, we would have found a way to completely vanquish it. (This was exactly the wrong approach to our conundrum!) But 1,4-dioxane endured, and in the rush to confront a never ending array of new challenges and opportunities, we never took a hard look at whether to publicly disclose the problem. In a sense, our 1,4-dioxane dilemma got "grandfathered in" under a new set of transparency rules. Predictably and painfully, it was soon revealed to the outside world. And those breathless headlines quickly followed.

I'd spent my entire career working to avoid just such an experience, but viewed another way, 1,4-dioxane presented us with an opportunity, albeit a rather extreme one, to learn what we'd discovered were new rules for transparency:

Rule 1: By exposing problems, transparency begins to solve them.
When a company begins to make itself transparent, it essentially embarks on an unblinking audit of all its activities. This process is similar to the lifecycle-analysis of a product. Just as a product-development team shines a spotlight on all the impacts of a new offering, from cradle to grave, the transparent company casts a bright light on itself as it measures all the systemic effects of its operations. The result is a 3-D picture of the organization's successes and, more importantly, its flaws and vulnerabilities. Only

by calculating and mapping its greatest negative effects can a company then develop strategies and policies for mitigating them. This process, though it sounds straightforward, runs against the grain of conventional business wisdom. It is scary, discomforting, and not what most business people are prepared for.

Soon after the 1,4-dioxane story broke, we launched a companywide effort to uncover any additional issues that consumers should know about, but don't. One such challenge involves our ongoing effort to find naturally-derived pigments for the dyes in our diaper products. This past April, we used the forum section of our website to engage consumers on the diaper-dye story. More stories will undoubtedly follow. Achieving greater transparency is a revolutionary goal but an iterative process. It starts with bringing inside-the-company conversations outside to the wider community.

A company can't be truly transparent if its community—its suppliers, manufacturers, and even its competitors—remains opaque. In our increasingly connected global world, companies are finding themselves enmeshed in larger ecosystems, where the actions of one entity reflect on all the others in the larger whole.

Some big brands in the U.S. apparel industry learned this first-hand a decade ago when child-labor violations in distant factories affected their reputations and, for a time, their performance. That's why we are attempting to exert a gravitational pull on companies in our orbit—and beyond—to help them meet the transparency challenge. Greater transparency is the first step toward taking greater responsibility for the future that all of us are creating.

Rule 2: As companies become transparent, demands for greater transparency increase.

With more and more employees and even CEOs starting to blog, and with activist groups and citizen stakeholders doing the same, the impulse (and the pressure) to publicly air company business grows stronger by the day. For any organization that aspires to create value by competing on values, it's doubly important to let the sun shine not only on its accomplishments, but also on its less-than-flattering secrets and failures. Stakeholders expect "good companies" to be open, candid, and engaged. Those expectations will snowball, whether we like it or not. (I like it!)

Up until several years ago, for example, no U.S. company would have dreamt of listing its subcontracting factories in developing countries on its website. Then Nike broke that taboo. Now it's an issue that every company with a global supply chain needs to consider and something that transparent companies have to think about even more. And pressures like these are always growing for businesses that wisely choose transparency.

For example, Seventh Generation does not disclose the names of its shareholders or the salaries of its employees, but will we *never* reveal this information? I don't know. If another company chooses to do so, there will certainly be pressure on us to follow suit.

I do know that the digital world's accelerating influence is rapidly destroying every organization's ability to completely manage its message. The rules are changing by the week, and as we learned from our 1,4-dioxane experience, it behooves any values-driven company to continually reassess its position relative to transparency. The ante just keeps getting higher.

Rule 3: Transparency is a process, not a prophecy.
Seventh Generation has for many years pushed to make itself more of a "see-through" organization, particularly with regard to labeling. While full ingredient disclosure is not required for cleaning products, we believe it's expected of us, and we voluntarily disclose both our ingredients and their health effects. Other brands are beginning to follow our lead.

Still, I don't know if we will ever be *sufficiently* transparent. It may be an unattainable goal, because society's expectations of what it means to be transparent undergo constant revision. The moment you think you have "arrived," you have failed. Transparency is not a state of being. It's an endless process of becoming.

No company that I am aware of lives entirely in a glass house and accepts the transparency challenge at every level of the organization. Some secrets—Coke's formula, Apple's design process, Cisco's M&A strategy—will probably remain unrevealed for quite some time. Yet, in a world where revelations of a company's business only fuels stakeholder hunger for more, transparency is unquestionably a business imperative.

It's not, however, for the faint-of-heart. No matter how committed we are to being open and accountable, we will always run into issues that are difficult to discuss. That said, I can assure you that as painful as it is to disclose a misstep or mistake, it hurts far more when an outside agent does it for you!

What's true of transparency is likewise true of our effort to succeed in the marketplace *and* contribute to society while also influencing other enterprises to contribute as well. It's a challenging and sometimes bewildering odyssey that tests the spirit and the will of each and every one of us. Over all, I am pleased with our progress to date. But never satisfied. As always, the journey continues...

Rule 4: It's personal

Transparency is not just about products, factories, and environmental impacts. It's also about who we are and how we do what we do. It's about sharing what you're working on, where things are going well and where they're not, and sharing not just our successes but our failures. Failures that are hidden from daylight often only help ensure that others will make the same mistakes. They deprive us of a dialogue with co-workers about what to do differently next time.

Transparency is about the beliefs we have about what we do, say, and think. It is about the assumptions we make and the uncertainties that keep us up at night.

I am an endlessly imperfect person, and transparency about those imperfections is an essential part of what makes me who I am. The fact that I enjoy the occasional steak, often drive too fast, live in a house that's bigger than I really need, or have a collection of more socks than I could ever wear is not something I need to hide.

At Seventh Generation transparency is what makes us an authentic brand and a trusted company. It's often painful and nerve-wracking, but our willingness to expose those things that most other businesses work so hard to hide is what makes us who we are. We don't get to choose when we're transparent. Instead, those decisions are made for us through an understanding of what it is that our partners and stakeholders expect us to share, and what they feel they need to know in order to maintain their trust.

In addition to increasing stakeholder trust and simply being the right thing to do, transparency also offers a critical competitive advantage. We live in a world desperate for things people can believe in and companies we can trust and depend upon. Yet most other companies simply don't believe in radical transparency. Instead they depend upon lawyers, accountants, and marketing research to tell them what to say and what to hide.

At Seventh Generation, we live in a much simpler world with one easy rule: Always tell the whole truth and nothing but the truth.

Chapter 12
The Art of Managing Intangible Assets

Fortune Magazine has calculated that 75% of the value of the average American company is represented by intangible assets.

12.1 Human Capabilities, Relationships, Brand, and Reputation

In December 2003, the World Economic Forum, whose membership is primarily drawn from the world's 1,000 leading global companies, sent a survey to participants in the organization's 34th Annual Meeting in Davos, Switzerland. One of the questions asked respondents what they thought was the most important measure of a company's success. 24% rated corporate reputation as most important. That answer was followed by profitability (17%), return on investment (13%), sustainability (6%), and stock market performance (5%). Only the quality of products or services (27%) trumped corporate reputation as the leading success measure.

The lead sentence of a Barron's September 12, 2005 cover story reads "For large companies, respect must be earned over decades, but it can be lost in an instant." Barron's own ratings of the world's most respected companies gives equal weight to competitive edge, consistent sales, profit growth, and ethical business practice.

Yet, intangible assets are almost completely overlooked by standard accounting principles. They don't show up in any systematic way on the balance sheet or on profit-loss statements. Intangibles, in other words, are not only intangible they are largely invisible where standard business management tools and disclosures are concerned.

Intangible Assets are rooted in human capabilities and are manifested in the relationships companies have with their consumers and supply chain. "They depend," writes Alan White in the BSR Business Brief *Intangibles and CSR*, "primarily on human creativity, not materials, and are transformed into enduring value for organizations by building know-how, capacity to innovate, and forming alliances and networks all which lead to enhancing brand and reputation. In less technical terms, intangibles have been described as the assets of an organization that remain after plant, equipment and inventory is sold, the lights have been turned off, and doors locked."

More and more companies have been investing in these kinds of assets. Indeed, in 1997, investment in intangibles (e.g., brand, training, R&D, etc.) exceeded investment in traditional tangibles (e.g., property, plant, equipment) for the first time. Today total investment in intangibles is estimated to be about $1 trillion per year. One need only observe the price-to-earnings and/or market-to-book ratios of companies like Microsoft, Google, and Starbucks to see how intangibles have begun to dominate to the creation of brand value.

Yet even in the face of often overwhelming evidence, little progress has been made in articulating and quantifying the impact and importance of intangible assets. Indeed, while virtually every CEO is quick to point to human capital as their organization's primary asset, it is typically this asset that is first in line to feel the consequences of mergers, acquisitions, and cost cutting. People and other intangibles simply aren't seen or measured as crucial forms of capital.

The current dominant view of capital as a hard-assets-only proposition is in many ways an outgrowth of the limited and skewed view of the purpose of the corporation. The ascendance of shareholder primacy during the last quarter century has obscured the pivotal role of non-financial capital. This focus on shareholders diverts attention from the fact that both the efficiency and the quantity of production increasingly depend on organizational variables—the specific ways in which human beings and technology are brought together to yield products and services. The traditional concept of capital masks the fundamental point that human beings and their networks of interrelations are, in fact, society's principal means of wealth creation. When done well, CSR strengthens and is strengthened by this recognition.

The perpetuation of the financial-centric view of capital is explained in large measure by its appealing simplicity. There's a lot to like about a system in which "all" company assets can be elegantly reduced to a short series of number that a 10 year-old could add up on a calculator.

The business world's narrow definition of capital also persists thanks to a great inertia that arises from the fact that those who manage this particular form of capital are the same as those who benefit from its continued dominance. This dominance is embedded in the perceived wisdom that financial capital rises above all other forms of capital as the key to an organization's value. While this once appeared to be true in the contemporary world of finance, we now know that even there it represents a vast and dangerous illusion. From the vantage point of sustainable development, the myth that the only legitimately meaningful form of capital is financial stands as a fundamental obstacle on the road to creating a system that would allow businesses to generate positive results for responsible behavior.

Yet as much as this bias obstructs progress, it also represents an enormous opportunity for CSR because it is a clear target that when hit will yield maximum benefits across a wide range of indicators. Expanding the common understanding of capital to include a wealth of intangibles lies at the heart of this challenge.

12.2 The Value Of Nature

For businesses to become sustainable, intangible assets must be valued and managed. There are other assets that must be treated with respect as well, specifically the natural resources that companies consume and depend upon. While businesses generally understand that their internal intangible assets have at least some value, natural resources are for the most part either undervalued or simply not valued at all.

Human society benefits from nature in countless ways. From aesthetic and spiritual benefits to cultural and communal functions, nature creates many kinds of value that are often hard to define. Nature also provides services that are essential to human life. These include ecological services like climate regulation, soil formation, and nutrient cycling as well as direct benefits like foods, fuels, fibers, and pharmaceuticals.

In the face of increasing human pressures on the environment, the irreplaceability of these and many other benefits *should* act as a powerful incentive to value, protect, and conserve the natural world, yet valuing these assets has historically been difficult because their true worth is generally not captured by conventional, market-based economic analyses.

Recently, the University of Vermont's Gund Institute for Ecological Economics embarked on a project to correct this longstanding accounting shortcoming and quantify the economic value of nature's goods and services. A 2006 article in the weekly Vermont paper Seven Days reported the initiative:

> "Imagine assigning a monetary value to bees pollinating a meadow. Or assessing the economic value of wetlands that provide critical habitat to endangered species and prevent coastal communities from being flooded. Right now, a logging company can put a price tag on a forest's uncut timber, and a real estate agent can assess the fair market value of undeveloped fields. But neither can measure, in actual dollars and cents, what those undisturbed ecosystems are worth in terms of the human benefits they already provide.

> "University of Vermont's Gund Institute for Ecological Economics has launched an ambitious new project to assign monetary values to all the world's ecosystems based on the natural functions they perform—from regulating climate to purifying water, replenishing soil to providing recreational opportunities. The science of 'ecosystem services' is revolutionizing the field of conservation by giving environmentalists and land-use planners tools for factoring nature into the cost of doing business. Ultimately, they hope, it will marshal the forces of the marketplace to encourage sustainable human activities and discourage unsustainable ones.

> "The project is the brainchild of Robert Costanza, founder and director of the Gund Institute. In May 1997, he published a now-famous article in the journal Nature in which he argues that, because the Earth's natural life-support systems contribute to human welfare, they represent a significant portion of the world's total economic worth. Costanza estimates the combined value of the world's

ecosystems at about $33 trillion per year, in current U.S. dollars. For comparison, the combined gross national product of all the world's countries totals about $18 trillion per year.

"Historically, economists and environmentalists have been averse to assigning monetary values to those things often described as 'God's creation,' Constanza explains. The traditional business model holds that, because such resources as clean air and clean water aren't manufactured or owned by anyone and can be accessed for little or no cost, they have no monetary worth. The benefits they provide—to companies, cities, states, or countries—are considered 'externalities' that needn't be factored into anyone's bottom line.

"Academically, the idea isn't as radical or controversial as it might seem, Costanza argues, since economists have long acknowledged the concept of externalities. 'It's just politically controversial because you're now saying, 'Here's something that you've been getting for free. This is something you've been stealing from the public, and now you've got to pay for it,' he adds."

12.3 They Spend. We Pay: The Crime of Externalized Costs

Though nature is clearly an intangible asset for the planet, the human race, and all of its businesses, it does not appear on anyone's balance sheet. As a result, we are free to use, abuse, consume, and destroy it with no financial consequences. And we do, thanks to a phenomenon called cost externalization that has been tacitly blessed by both governments and the accounting profession.

David Korten, a lifelong opponent of externalized costs, describes the process this way in his book *When Corporations Rule the World*:

"(A) basic condition of efficient market allocation is that the full costs of production must be borne by the producer and be included in the producer's selling price. Economists call it cost internalization. If some portion of the cost of producing a product are borne by third parties who in no way participate in or benefit from the transaction, then economists say the costs have been externalized and the price of the product is distorted accordingly. Another way of putting it is that every externalized cost involves privatizing a gain and socializing its associated costs onto the community.

"Externalized costs don't go away—they are simply ignored by those who benefit from making the decisions that result in others incurring them. For example, when a forest products corporation obtains rights to clear-cut Forest Service land at give away prices and leaves behind a devastated habitat, the company reaps the immediate profit and the society bears the long term cost.

"Similarly, Dow Chemical externalizes production costs when it dumps wastes without adequate treatment, thus passing the resulting costs of air, water, and soil pollution onto the community in the form of additional health costs, discomfort, lost working days, a need to buy bottled water, and the cost of cleaning up what has been contaminated. Wal-Mart externalizes costs when it buys from Chinese contractors who pay their workers too little to maintain their basic physical and mental health or fail to maintain adequate worker safety standards and then dismiss without compensation those workers who are injured.

"When the seller retains the benefit of the externalized cost, this represents an unearned profit—an important source of market inefficiency. Passing the benefit to the buyer in the form of a lower price creates still another source of inefficiency by encouraging forms of consumption that use finite resources inefficiently. For example, the more the environmental and social costs of producing and driving an automobile are externalized [as a result, for example, of inefficient cars that generate air pollution that adversely effects public health, the costs of which are borne by society, not by the driver of the car or the manufacturer of the automobile], the more automobiles people buy and the more they drive them. Urban sprawl increases, more of our productive lands are paved over, more pollutants are released, petroleum reserves are depleted more rapidly, and voters favor highway construction over public transportation, sidewalks, and bicycle paths.

"Market forces create substantial pressure on business to decrease costs and increase profits by increasing efficiency. The corporate rationalists fail to mention that one way firms increase their 'efficiency' is to externalize more of their costs. The more powerful the firm, the greater its ability to take this course."

The externalization of costs, though a tradition that's become deeply imbedded in our economy, is unsustainable. It leads businesses to make decisions that deliver short-term profits at the expense of their very survival and our own as well. Yet this is understandable. Why, given the legal opportunity to ignore an expense and enjoy additional profit as a result, would any corporation forgo externalizing any and all possible costs?

The good news is that a variety of companies, driven by the same pressures and opportunities that are causing them to embed corporate responsibility and sustainability practices into their business, are beginning to address the cost externalization issue.

Many leading businesses are responding to the fact that there are increasingly greater risks to not taking responsibility for externalized costs, risks that range from damage to brand reputation to outright legal jeopardy. These firms are voluntarily taking responsibility for these costs by either internalizing or, better yet, simply eliminating them. Examples of this trend include Honda's focus on engineering its entire automobile portfolio to generate less CO_2 emissions than any other car company; Timberland's elimination of glues and leather tanning practices that expose workers to toxic fumes; and Patagonia's switch to 100% organic cotton for all the clothing it sells.

The process of measuring and eliminating externalities is one that's both time consuming and expensive. At Seventh Generation, we spend $50,000 to $100,000 a year on the task, and large public companies are easily spending a million dollars or more, a figure that does not include the costs of remediating negative effects already created.

Such calculations are at best incomplete because in many cases there are no standards or agreed upon measures to make them. If a polluter is responsible for an increase in the asthma or cancer rate in their community, what cost should they be assessed? If pollution reduces the trout population in the stream that runs behind your home, what fee should the polluter be charged?

With wide open questions like these still in search of legitimate answers, it's no wonder that no business can yet claim a 100% success rate when it comes to internalizing previously externalized costs. Still, it's important that every company begin to work toward this fundamentally necessary goal.

That work begins with documentation of externalized costs through a process of sustainability reporting designed by the Global Reporting Initiative (GRI).[10] This report should capture a significant amount of a company's environmental footprint and much of its "social" footprint as possible.[11] By social footprint, I mean the social costs that the company is passing along to the greater community. For example, the effect that Wal-Mart might have on a town or a state by not offering adequate health insurance to its employees, an externalization which forces uninsured workers to frequent hospital emergency rooms for care that is effectively paid for by local taxpayers.

This process is further complicated because even among environmental economists like Robert Costanza and the Gund Institute there's no real consensus on where responsibilities begin or end. While most believe that these responsibilities should span a product's complete life cycle and run from the extraction of the raw materials needed to manufacture it to the impacts created by its eventual end-of-life disposal, there's no agreement on who should pay for the negative effects that result from using the product.

At Seventh Generation, even though we attempt to make these calculations, the impacts are not easy to quantify and they are often counter intuitive as we discovered in our 1993/1994 CSR Report when we evaluated the life cycle of our laundry products.

We had decided to examine the greenhouse gases (GHGs) emitted at key stages in the life cycle of our liquid laundry detergent in order to learn which parts of that life cycle have the greatest impact on global warming. We studied all major impact categories, including surfactant manufacture, packaging, transportation, consumer use, and wastewater treatment. The results were startling to say the least.

After conducting all kinds of analyses, we discovered that an extraordinary 96% of all GHG emissions related to the manufacturing, use, and disposal of our laundry products occurred when consumers used them. That's because these products were being used in warm or hot water, and heating this water resulted in the production of the lion's share of GHGs.

While our substitution of plant-based surfactants for petroleum-based surfactants does provide some GHG benefits, our complete set of life-cycle data showed us that the biggest positive impact we could engineer by far would come from getting our consumers to use lower wash temperatures.[12]

As a result of this newfound knowledge, we developed a liquid laundry detergent specifically formulated for cold water use in today's new generation of energy efficient washers. We have also begun educating consumers on the environmental benefits of washing more laundry in cold or warm water.

As this case study aptly illustrates, we can learn surprising and useful things by documenting externalized costs. Once this initial process has been completed, the next step is to prioritize the internalization of these costs and develop an action plan.

This can be challenging because often one ends up comparing apples and oranges. For example, what's worse: air pollution or water pollution? It's a good question and one without an easy answer.

Since you can't attack all the externalized cost challenges at once, you need to make transparent choices driven by a set of beliefs so that stakeholders can engage you in dialogue around these decisions. In our own case, Seventh Generation made greenhouse gases a priority in 2006, a choice that made other issues like water use and biodiversity secondary focuses.

No matter what externalized aspect you choose to focus on, however, it's important to remember that little can be accomplished without engaging your supply chain. Indeed, it is often their willingness to partner with you that will have the greatest effect on the rate of progress you can make.

Setting measurable goals is the next step in the process. As a Board member of Greenpeace, I know that no matter how egregious we might find a particular corporate practice, we must acknowledge that change takes time, and we must summon the patience needed while it comes. We can't demand instant change. Instead Greenpeace, as well as most other

NGOs, looks for a commitment to change over a reasonable period of time. Though we can argue over how fast is fast enough, an open dialogue will usually land us somewhere in the middle of the spectrum of possibility.

The last part of the process is unquestionably the most challenging: figuring out how to finance a change to a product or formulation, a retooling of a factory or transportation fleet, the switch to a more sustainable energy source, or the education and training required to proactively manage the whole process. While in some cases such changes have relatively short returns on investment, as has been the case with the "greening" of Wal-Mart's fleet of trucks or the construction of LEED-certified buildings, in many cases, like the redesign of an assembly line for closed loop manufacturing, the search for cost effective solutions takes creativity, systems-based thinking, and often the help of outside experts.

Chapter 13

Our Customers Are No Longer Consumers

Dear Seventh Generation,

I'm e-mailing you because my heart has been overflowing with gratitude for your company since Saturday night. I was emptying the dishwasher, my fifteen month old daughter was playing with the dishwasher door and, being exhausted, what she was doing wasn't registering with me. Then I looked down, and saw that she had two handfuls and a mouthful of your dishwashing powder. The dishwasher had malfunctioned, the little door on the door that disperses the dishwashing powder hadn't opened during the wash, it was all still in there, and my daughter had opened it while I wasn't paying attention. She'd shoved a ton into her mouth.

Frantic, I called Poison Control. "My daughter ate dishwashing powder." They asked what brand it was. "Seventh Generation." "Oh, it's fine then. Just wash it off her hands, and give her a glass of water."

I shudder to think about the different night we would have had if it had been one of the many toxic dishwashing powders with chlorine in them. We'd have probably had to call 911 and been ambulanced down the mountain we live on.

I'm bcc:ing this to my friends and family who have children, grandchildren, and who are trying to and going to have children soon because I see how vital it is to have nontoxic products around the house—to protect the environment our kids will live in all their lives, and to prevent accidents that could cut short our children's lives. Our family uses so many of your products. I am so grateful to you for Saturday night. "Price of Seventh Generation products—not much. That of a Saturday night with a happy, healthy, alive child...priceless."

Thank you, thank you, thank you!

Sincerely, Gabrielle Lennon

As testimonials go, it just doesn't get any better than this. But this recent e-mail is more than a simple love letter written by a grateful customer. It's real-world validation of a very important piece of wisdom we should all take to heart: Our customers are no longer mere consumers. They are our brand.

Harvey Hartman, founder of the Hartman Group, visited us some years ago to and taught us this important lesson about our brand and its position in the marketplace. In doing so, he shattered our illusions about the importance of what we do and think about day in and day out.

"Your brand doesn't live within the walls of your offices," he said. "It lives in the minds and hopefully the hearts of your customers. All that matters is what they think and say about Seventh Generation. While you have some influence with them, their experience of your brand *is* the brand. What they tell their friends matters much more than whatever you say in an advertisement or on your website. I hope you're listening carefully."

Harvey is right. Consumers own and control the fate of our brand. And they can do more than that if we let them. They'll provide ideas for new products and content for our website. They'll create local publicity and share valuable information they get from us with everyone they know. To build a business that will thrive in the future, we must meet the needs of our customers in ways that transcend the form and function that most products are designed to fulfill. Successful brands will support their customers in their quest to live the lives that they want to live and be the people they seek to become.

Most companies, however, don't think about their own success in this way. Instead, they use the entirely wrong framework, one that measures success by how few people complain about their products and services, not by how many people they delight.

In the book *The Support Economy: Why Corporations Are Failing Individuals And The Next Episode Of Capitalism,* authors Shoshana Zuboff and James Maxmin articulate the growing divide between our aspirations and needs as individuals and the products and services most companies provide. In an interview on their website they discuss the essence of their point of view.

"People's desires, needs, and wants have radically changed, but corporations have remained distant and indifferent to the true nature of this change. As a result, we have a business environment in which people are chronically disappointed and frustrated by their experiences as consumers and employees. We no longer trust large organizations to serve our needs. On every level, we are experiencing a divisive 'us vs. them' mentality. Now, after decades of being forced to put up with the consequences of corporate indifference, individual end consumers are striking out on their own to blaze new trails in a new approach to consumption that we call the individuation of consumption.

"People want to be treated as individuals, not as anonymous transactions in the ledgers of mass consumption. They want to be heard and they want to matter. They no longer want to be the objects of commerce. Instead, they want corporations to bend to their needs. They want to be freed from the time-consuming stress, rage, injustice, and personal defeat that accompany so many commercial exchanges. They seek advocacy in place of adversarialism, relationships in place of transactions. They want to take their lives in their own hands and they are willing to pay for what we call the deep support that will enable them to do so.

"Deep support is not just an enhanced version of conventional customer service. It is an entirely new way of doing business, a radically different approach to the realization of value in which the very purpose of commerce is redefined around the objective of supporting individuals.

"Deep support enables psychological self-determination. It produces time for life. It facilitates and enhances the experience of being the origin of one's life. It recognizes, responds to, and promotes individuality. It celebrates intricacy. It multiplies choice and enhances flexibility. It encourages voice and is guided by voice. Deep support listens and offers connection. It offers collaborative relationship defined by advocacy. It is founded on trust, reciprocity, authenticity, intimacy, and absolute reliability."

That may seem like a tall order, and it is; building these types of relationships is no easy matter. In many respects it requires not just a new type of company with enlightened leadership but a whole new way of thinking.

Because in today's world, brands can no longer be built on the simplistic traditional foundation of advertising, promotions, coupons, and free product samples. Instead successful brands are built through dialogue, relationship, discovery, and mutual support. These "new" brands create deep and lasting relationships with their consumers, and as a result they become something more essential in their buyers' lives than a mere product.

At Seventh Generation, the way we partner with our consumers in the pursuit of our global imperatives creates a bond that no 30-second TV ad or sweepstakes contest can duplicate. Rather than try to build customer loyalty and trust by simply screaming louder than everyone else in the marketplace, our consumers are invited into our brand and encouraged to stay and participate. This approach is one that works more slowly than conventional consumer loyalty strategies—our consumers discover our essence over time as they learn about us via initiatives in which we are true to ourselves, like WAGES, Change-It, and Tampontification. This slower, quieter approach, however, results in a much deeper and more permanent relationship,

At Seventh Generation, we aspire to help lead, design, and model these new relationships by being a company that views its customers as partners in a series of shared quests and not simply consumers of the products we make. We see the purchase of our products as just the first link in a long chain of mutual trust and support that ends, we hope, with the fulfillment of the dreams and aspirations of each of us no matter what our original roles as sellers or buyers.

As an employee of Seventh Generation, you have a critical part to play in the care and feeding of this new kind of commerce and a central role in the nurturing of the brand and the customers that together are allowing us make it a reality. The good news is that the cultivation of our unique consumer stakeholder relationships can be a simple thing for each of us to achieve. All we have to do is treat and respect our customers, and indeed all of our stakeholders, as we ourselves wish to be treated.

Appendix A
Global Imperatives

(Original Draft – April 3, 2006)

1. Businesses (particularly, but not exclusively) are educators and provisioners of a conscious enlightened citizenry enabling them to use their decisions and actions to create equity and justice via the market place. Business leaders rise to the challenge of being internally and externally committed to all their actions producing conscious workers, citizens, and consumers.

2. Businesses consciously affect their own direction such that they align with planetary and social imperatives.

3. Holding the present and the future in the same mind, businesses produce a world rich in value as contrasted to a world rich in artifacts and devoid of resources that is appropriate to health and wellbeing for all.

4. Efforts are pursued to increase the correlation between real and lasting value and performance. There is no contradiction between short and long term goals, performance and understanding.

5. Governance and social systems pursue deeper and increasingly meaningful levels of providing for future security of all beings and increasing the capacity for understanding differing perspectives that develop systems of peace, equity, justice, and love for all planetary beings.

6. Business engages all people in personal development toward higher levels of consciousness such that they aspire and con-

tribute to improving the viability and vitality of life-affirming value-adding processes of all living systems.

7. Individual and group effort continuously reflect upon how effectively they are consciously engaging in pursuits which enable larger wholes to fulfill their developmental potential.

8. All products, product offerings, byproducts, and processes (the products life cycle) are restorative, enhancing the potential of all the systems they touch, both natural and human. If those natural systems have evolutionary potential, we will awaken and develop our understanding of the systems and their potential so that we and our products life cycle can partner in the evolutionary process.

9. Ensure that globally, natural resources are used and renewed at a rate that is always below their rate depletion. We live within the limits of this rate of exchange between humans and planetary systems, supporting the earth's capacity to evolve itself to new levels of realization.

Appendix B
The Inspired Protagonist's Reading List

As you know, much of my inspiration and many of the ideas found in this book are drawn from the work of some of the world's leading environmental thinkers and business management visionaries. These people are not merely occupying today's progressive cutting edge. They are creating it via a series of far-ranging new theories and perspectives that are transforming our world.

The bad news is that we don't have space here to do much more than scratch the surface of their innumerable insights. The good news is that you can get to the heart of the many important things they have to say by reading some or all of the works I've highlighted in this appendix.

These are the key books that have illuminated my own path to enlightenment, and I highly recommend reading as many of them as you possibly can. Together, they create a kind of road map to where it is that we want to go. Having them in your metaphorical pack on the journey ahead will only make it easier to get there and more rewarding when we do.

The Bridge at the Edge of the World: Capitalism, the Environment, and Crossing From Crisis to Sustainability
James Gustave Speth, Yale University Press, 2008

James Gustave Speth, co-founder of the NRDC, Yale University dean, and former White House advisor, has written a great book that everyone concerned with the fate of the world must read.

Speth takes business, government, NGO's, individuals, and the capitalist system at large to task in this urgent appeal to make large scale, fundamental changes to the path we are on. More than most, Speth attacks the incremental nature of change—from the corporate responsibility movement to the environmental arena—as woefully and dangerously inadequate.

The book is compelling, deeply thoughtful, thoroughly researched, and a pleasure (albeit a depressing one) to read. My only complaint is that while Speth identifies the key trends that will be part of the solution, he stops short of detailing their implementation, something we desperately need in order to catalyze urgent movement toward action.

NPR described the book as a "monumental work of synthesis" and in an interview noted that Speth has, "marshaled formidable evidence that American-style consumer capitalism of the early twenty-first century is incompatible with maintaining quality of life for all of us. It is generating unprecedented environmental risks while failing to advance the happiness and social well-being of Americans."

Specifically Speth proposes that:

"We must change the very nature of corporations so they become legally accountable to society at large, not just to themselves and their shareholders. We must challenge the current obsession with GDP growth and focus on growth in the areas that truly enhance human well-being: growth in good jobs, in the availability of health care, in education, in the deployment of green technologies, in the incomes of the poor, in security against illness and disability, in infrastructure, and more. We must challenge materialism and consumerism as the source of happiness and seek new values about quality of life, social solidarity, and connectedness to nature. We must transform the market through government action so that it works for the environment, rather than against it. We must transform democracy through deep political reforms that reassert popular control, encouraging locally strong, deliberative democracy and limiting corporate influence. We must forge a new environmental politics that recognizes links among environmentalism, social liberalism, human and civil rights, the fight against poverty, and other issues."

I completely agree. And while Speth's analysis and recommendations demand a lot of us, we should all be thankful that someone, at last is willing to say, "Hey we're in deep shit here, and if we aren't willing to do the hard work needed to get it together there will be dire consequences for us all. It is NOT going to be easy to be green and ensure the viability of most of the human race on the planet. But we damn well better start trying right now."

The Big Squeeze: Tough Times for the American Worker
Steven Greenhouse, Knopf, 2008

After reading this look at the treatment of the American worker, you will never again feel the same way about using the services of FedEx (a company I once held in pretty high regard). You may never shop in Circuit City, fly Northwest Airlines, buy groceries at A&P, get your haircut at Smart-Style or have lunch at Taco Bell.

But let's start with a short excerpt that will show the kinds of eye-opening things this book reveals. It's about Wal-Mart, a company whose untapped potential to become a force for good I've been trying pretty hard to keep believing in.

> "In his job at a Wal-Mart in Texas, Mike Michell was responsible for catching shoplifters, and he was good at it, too, catching 180 in one two-year period. But one afternoon things went wildly awry when he chased a thief—a woman using stolen checks—into the parking lot. She jumped into her car, and her accomplice gunned the accelerator, slamming the car into Michell and sending him to the hospital with a broken kneecap, a badly torn shoulder, and two herniated disks. Michell was so devoted to Wal-Mart that he somehow returned to work the next day, but a few weeks later he told his boss that he needed surgery on his knee. He was fired soon afterward, apparently as part of a strategy to dismiss workers whose injuries run up Wal-Mart's workers' comp bills."

We all keep hearing that times are tough, competition is brutal, and low wage developing countries are eating our businesses for lunch. But if that's the case, why have corporate profits soared, climbing on average 13 percent a year for the six years, while wages have remained flat?

Greenhouse writes that:

"Employee productivity has outpaced wages, rising 15 percent from 2001 through 2007. Corporate profits have climbed to their highest share of national income in sixty-four years, while the share going to wages has sunk to its lowest level since 1929. 'This is the most pronounced several years of labor's share declining,' said Lawrence Katz, an economics professor at Harvard. 'For as long as we've had a modern economy, this is the worst we've seen it.' Very simply, corporations, along with their CEOs, are seizing a bigger piece of the nation's economic pie for themselves, leaving the nation's workers and their families diminished."

Well, we've heard that before. But what we haven't heard are the stories of how the headlines play out in people's lives. What it feels like to be laid off, for example, by Northwest Airlines and receive a booklet titled "101 Ways to Save Money," that suggests ex-employees not "be shy about pulling something you like out of the trash."

Capitalism As If the World Matters
Jonathan Porritt, Earthscan, 2005

This book is essential for anyone seeking to understand the essentials of developing a sustainable economy. Porritt is chairman of the UK Sustainable Development Commission, former chairman of the Ecology Party (now the Green Party), a former director of the Friends of the Earth UK, and currently runs the Forum for the Future, which aims to persuade individual businesses to improve their environmental performance, and he knows of what he speaks.

"With great respect to those who assert the so-called 'primacy' of key social and economic goals (such as the elimination of poverty or the attainment of universal human rights), it must be said loud and clear that these are secondary goals: all else is conditional upon learning to live sustainably within the Earth's systems and limits. Not only is the pursuit of biophysical sustainability non-negotiable; it's preconditional.

Having said that, these are really two sides of the same coin. On the one hand, social sustainability is entirely dependent upon ecological sustainability. As we continue to undermine nature's capacity to provide humans with essential services (such as clean water, a stable climate and so on) and resources (such as food and raw materials), both individuals and nation states will be subjected to growing amounts of pressure. Conflict will grow, and threats to public health and personal safety will increase in the face of ecological degradation."

Creating a World Without Poverty: Social Business and the Future of Capitalism
Muhammad Yunus, PublicAffairs, 2008

An economics professor and winner of the 2007 Nobel Peace Prize, Yunus says he originally became involved in poverty not as a policy-maker, scholar, or researcher, but because poverty was all around him. With these words he stopped teaching elegant theories and began lending small amounts of money, $40 or less, without collateral to the poorest women in the world.

Thirty-three years later, the Grameen Bank has helped seven million people live better lives by building businesses to serve the poor. The bank is solidly profitable, with a 98.6% repayment rate. It inspired the micro-credit movement, which has helped 100 million of the poorest people in the world escape poverty, and it earned Yunus the title "Banker to the Poor." His latest book recounts the story of microcredit and discusses Social Business, organizations designed to help people while turning profits. French food giant Danone's partnership to market yogurt in Bangladesh, which we discuss in this book, is described here in detail, along with 25 other businesses that operate under the Grameen banner. Infused with entrepreneurial spirit and the excitement of a worthy challenge, this book is the opposite of pessimistic recitals of intractable poverty's horrors.

The Black Swan
Nassim Nicholas Taleb, Random House, 2007

"My major hobby is teasing people who take themselves & the quality of their knowledge too seriously & those who don't have the guts to sometimes say: I don't know...

"You know what is wrong with a lot more confidence than what is right.

"How can we figure out the properties of the (infinite) unknown based on the (finite) known?"

—Nassim Nicholas Taleb

Every once in a while a book comes a long that jolts you awake, like a swift slap in the face after a wonderfully strong cup of coffee, and makes you rethink how you think and realize that if you want to think well you will need to be a lot more careful and intentional. The Black Swan is that book.

Unfortunately it's also a book that's impossible to describe without reproducing large portions of it.

The Guardian newspaper review asks one of its key questions: "Why are we so bad at acknowledging life's unpredictability? Things happen, and surprise us. Afterwards, we act as if they were explicable all along. Then we use those explanations to pretend we can control the future: act boldly, and you'll become rich; keep an eye on loners, and you'll prevent massacres. 'There's just much, much more luck than we think,' Taleb says."

For more about this extraordinary book, visit Taleb's website at www.fooledbyrandomness.com.

The Support Economy: Why Corporations Are Failing Individuals and The Next Episode Of Capitalism
Shoshana Zuboff and James Maxmin, Viking, 2002

This book articulates the growing divide between our aspirations and needs as individuals and the products and services most companies provide.

> "People's desires, needs, and wants have radically changed, but corporations have remained distant and indifferent to the true nature of this change. As a result, we have a business environment in which people are chronically disappointed and frustrated by their experiences as consumers and employees. We no longer trust large organizations to serve our needs. On every level, we are experiencing a divisive 'us vs. them' mentality. Now, after decades of being forced

to put up with the consequences of corporate indifference, individuals and consumers are striking out on their own to blaze new trails in a new approach to consumption that we call the individuation of consumption. They are pointing us toward the next leap forward in wealth creation that we call the support economy."

Revolutionary Wealth: How It Will Be Created and How It Will Change Our Lives
Alvin and Heidi Toffler, Currency/Doubleday, 2007

In their most recent book, the Tofflers describe a huge new and uncharted part of our economy they call "prosuming," the creation of "goods, services or experiences for our own use or satisfaction, rather than for sale or exchange," or the co-creation of a product or service offered by a third party or the participation in its delivery in a way that involves no direct financial compensation. This includes everything from parenting and caring for an elderly friend to building Wikipedia to providing self-banking services through the use of ATM's.

Presence
Peter M. Senge, C. Otto Scharmer, Joseph Jaworski, Betty S. Flowers, Bantam Dell Publishing Group, 2008

This is probably the best and most important book I've read in the last 10 years!

Unlike most of what I read, *Presence* was more like a wonderful meditation than a dose of information.

One quote I will probably never forget is "the longest road is often from your mind to your heart." It will forever remind me that more value will always come from love than from anything else. How can I do all that I do lovingly? As a serial entrepreneur, I am pretty good at action, criticism, analysis, and creativity. But I still have a lot to learn about love. One can of course be lovingly critical or analytical, but somehow the depth of my analysis usually seems greater than the depth of my love.

I was also overwhelmed with the notion of how much of our lives fall within the pre-established patterns we seem to follow over and over. Whether it's how we respond to each other, read the newspaper, participate in a meeting, or watch a sunset, most of what we do, we do as we have done before. Somehow the possibility of doing it differently doesn't occur to us. Outside our patterns is all the possibility. Whether it's figuring out how to stop global warming, be a better lover, or design a new product, 99% of what is possibility, but yet to be, lies outside the pattern.

If we can slow down our thinking enough to actually watch how we think, become conscious of the generation of our thoughts, question whether there is another way to see what we are seeing, do what we are doing, hold what we are holding, a whole new world opens up before us. That's the world to which *Presence* takes us. And it's a destination I hope you'll use this wonderful book to find.

Synchronicity: The Inner Path of Leadership
Joseph Jaworski and Betty S. Flowers, Berrett-Koehler Publishers, 1998

> "One of the most important roles we can play individually or collectively is to create an opening, or to 'listen' to the implicate order unfolding, and then to create dreams, visions, and stories that we sense at our center want to happen..."

This is the perfect way to continue the meditation that begins with *Presence*, which Jaworski co-wrote. The point of view put forth by Jaworski holds out the challenge, opportunity, and possibility found in a fundamentally new way to lead. Some excerpts:

> "True leadership is about creating a domain in which we continually learn and become more capable of participating in our unfolding future. A true leader thus sets the stage on which predictable miracles, synchronistic in nature, can—and do—occur.

> "The deeper territory of leadership (means) collectively 'listening' to what is wanting to emerge in the world, and then having the courage to do what is required.

"The entire past is enfolded in us in a very subtle way. If you reach deeply into yourself, you are reaching into the very essence of mankind.... We are all connected. If this could be taught, and if people could understand it, we would have a very different consciousness.... (P)eople create barriers between each other by their fragmentary thought. Each one operates separately. When these barriers have been dissolved, then there arises one mind...."

A Company of Citizens: What the World's First Democracy Teaches
Brook Manville and Josiah Ober, Harvard Business Press, 2003

This book presents a roadmap for business based in part on the participatory democratic system found in ancient Athens, which created the experience of a collective journey and shared responsibility.

One review of the book noted that "membership in the city's leadership was rotated among all citizens. Everyone's voice was welcome. The citizens and their community lived by a code that Manville and Ober describe as "moral reciprocity" which "provided the essential link between 'What's in it for me?' and 'What's in it for us?' (and eliminated) the conflict between self-interest and community interest. Manville and Ober contrast the open, inclusive environment of ancient Athens with the "closed doors of executive offices and conference rooms," where decisions are made by a small group of "insular elites." Indeed, "the entire shape of the modern company reflects a fundamental distrust of its members," the authors argue.

The Real Wealth of Nations: Creating a Caring Economics
Riane Eisler, Berrett-Koehler Publishers, 2007

Great books are few and far between, so go out and get this one. This review from the Baltimore Chronicle gives a better overview than I can:

"Do you ever open your eyes in the morning and think, Oh, wow, why bother...? If so, you'll be glad to hear that macrohistorian and cultural transformation theorist Riane Eisler has just delivered another massive and exhilarating dose of hope for the sane and weary, with the publication of her latest book, *The Real Wealth of Nations: Creating a Caring Economics.*

"In The *Chalice and the Blade*, her 1987 introduction to 'partnership' as the leitmotif of sane social engineering, Eisler persuasively argued that nonviolent, egalitarian, culturally advanced, and prosperous societies have existed in the past and could certainly be made (by us) to exist again."

"Now comes *The Real Wealth of Nations*, tackling the ominous gaps in our mental map of what economic theory is all about. An economy is more than the market, the government, and the military, says Eisler, eventually citing chapter and verse from a long list of other scholars to create a very persuasive case. A complete picture of a national and global economy must include the whole range of vital caring and caregiving activities—mostly undervalued, undercounted, and either severely underpaid or totally unpaid; and mostly performed (surprise!) by women—that take place in the community and in the home.

"Eisler, a meticulous cross-disciplinary researcher, presents a good deal of cheering evidence to fortify her recommendations. What we spend to maximize the value of so-called human capital, for example (i.e., caring for and educating our children and youth), should be considered not a burdensome expense but a capital investment, insists the author; and as such, it should be amortizable over twenty years—the time frame for nurturing a generation of healthy, high-performing human beings. To back that up, she presents research outcomes showing that, e.g., early childhood educational interventions produce a 200 percent return on investment, and that actual companies that have adopted a comprehensively caring orientation to their workforce more than recoup their considerable investment in health care, exercise facilities, onsite child care, parental leave, and so forth, with better motivated employees, lower turnover and training costs, and higher productivity.

"The cases cited come from enlightened regions like the Nordic nations, where social policy is light-years ahead of nearly everyone else's; but even in the USA, where the publicly funded social safety net now consists of way more holes than netting, there are already numerous companies profiting over the long term from this kind of investment in caring and caregiving.

"For about the price of a good vegan (or steak) dinner, you can order *The Real Wealth of Nations* in hardcover. This is one time when I wouldn't wait for the paperback edition. Your alarm will buzz again at the usual time tomorrow morning. As you open your eyes on another day of global warming, tribal and regional conflict, and general transnational chaos, it will feel wonderful to have Eisler on your team, sharing her straightforward prescription for planetary rescue: a lot more serious, high-level, long-range attention to the crucial economic role of caring and caregiving, and a thoroughly partnerist orientation, starting right now. Today."

The Market for Virtue: The Potential and Limits of Corporate Social Responsibility
David Vogel, Brookings Institution Press, 2006

Despite the powerful forces driving businesses to become better corporate citizens, the measurable impact of corporate responsibility in the marketplace, according to David Vogel, has been underwhelming. While select businesses have made big changes that have translated into superior financial performance, there is much left to be done. Vogel, a friend and occasional debating partner, has attempted to add up the total cumulative marketplace impact of thousands of activities in companies throughout the economy, and while the absolute numbers are small and somewhat depressing, I would note the trend is still just beginning.

The Market for Virtue explores the extent to which improvements in corporate conduct can occur without more extensive or effective government regulation. What is the long-term potential of this self-regulation? The improvement that can be expected is far more modest than recent breathless writing on CSR would indicate. At some point, many businesses must choose between doing what seems ethically right and what is most profitable. Since businesses are typically created to make money—and because shareholders and capitalism demand that they do so—the bottom line tends to win out. There is a market for virtue, but it is limited by the substantial costs of more responsible business behavior.

Wholeness and the Implicate Order
David Bohm, Routledge Press, 2002

This a book I aspire to finish reading some day. Bohm could be considered the grandfather of today's sustainability movement. He provides the philosophical underpinnings of modern systems thinking and writes about the essential interrelatedness and interdependence of all phenomena—physiological, social, and cultural. Nothing can be understood in isolation, everything has to be seen as part of a unified whole. It is only through abstraction that things look separate. We are each "the whole of mankind." That's the idea of the implicate order—that everything is enfolded in everything else.

Biomimicry: Innovation Inspired by Nature
Janine Benyus, Harper Perennial, 2002

Janine Benyus, one of sustainability's most brilliant minds, developed the idea of Biomimicry, the rather simple idea that if we can understand the way in which nature works to acquire and store energy, build bridges and tunnels, create community, and manage population we might get some clues as to what we need to do to create more sustainable businesses.

Benyus describes Biomimicry as "coming from bios, meaning life, and mimesis, meaning to imitate, and is a design discipline that studies nature's best ideas and then imitates these designs and processes to solve human problems. Studying a leaf to invent a better solar cell is an example of this "innovation inspired by nature."

Though Benyus has worked at the fringes of business, she has yet to breakthrough to the mainstream. There are few individuals more deserving of being discovered, however, than she is. "The core idea," she writes, "is that nature, imaginative by necessity, has already solved many of the problems we are grappling with. Animals, plants, and microbes are the consummate engineers. They have found what works, what is appropriate, and most important, what lasts here on Earth. This is the real news of biomimicry: After 3.8 billion years of research and development, failures are fossils, and what surrounds us is the secret to survival."

> "Like the viceroy butterfly imitating the monarch, we humans have at last begun to imitate the best and brightest organisms in our habitat. We are learning, for instance, how to grow food like a prairie, build ceramics like an abalone, create color like a peacock, self-medicate like a chimp, compute like a cell, and run a business like a hickory forest.

"The conscious emulation of life's genius is a survival strategy for the human race, a path to a sustainable future. The more our world looks and functions like the natural world, the more likely we are to endure on this home that is ours, but not ours alone."

Here are some other classic books on sustainable business and best practices that you may want to read as well:

Natural Capitalism: Creating the Next Industrial Revolution
Paul Hawken, Amory Lovins, and L. Hunter Lovins, Back Bay Books, 2000

Beyond Growth: The Economics of Sustainable Development
Herman E. Daly, Beacon Press Books, August 1997

Built to Last: Successful Habits of Visionary Companies
JC Collins and JI Porras, Random House, 1995

Cannibals With Forks: The Triple Bottom Line of 21st Century Business
John Elkington, Capstone, 1997

The Chrysalis Economy, How Citizen CEOs and Corporations Can Fuse Values and Value Creation
John Elkington, Capstone Publishing Ltd, 2001

The Civil Corporation: The New Economy of Corporate Citizenship
Simon Zadek, Earthscan Publications Ltd, 2001

Corporate Citizenship
Malcolm McIntosh, Deborah Leipziger, Keith Jones and Gill Coleman, Financial Times and Pittman Publishing, 1998

Cradle to Cradle: Remaking the Way We Make Things
William McDonough and Michael Braungart, North Point Press, 2002

Value Shift: Why Companies Must Merge Social and Financial Imperatives to Achieve Superior Results
Lynn Sharp Paine, McGraw Hill, 2002

Endnotes

1 Neil Chamberlain, *The Limits of Corporate Responsibility*, Basic Books, 1973, p. 4

2 John Elkington, *Cannibals With Forks: The Triple Bottom Line of 21st Century Business*, New Society Publishers, 1998, p. ix

3 *Private Authority and International Relations*, A. Claire Cutler, Virginia Hafler, and Tony Porter, eds., Albany: State University of New York Press, 1999, p. 213

4 The former critique comes from the left. See for example, D. Korten, *When Corporations Rule The World*, Kumarian, 1997 and Joel Bakan, *The Corporation: The Pathological Pursuit of Power*, The Free Press, 2004. The latter comes from the right. See for example, Benjamin Hunt, *The Timid Corporation; Why Business is Terrified of Taking Risk*, London, Wiley, 2003 and David Henderson, *Misguided Virtue: False Notions of Corporate Responsibility*, New Zealand Business Roundtable, June 2001

5 This phenomena is explored in Michele Micheletti, *Political Virtue and Shopping*, Palgrave Macmillan, 2003 and David Vogel, *Lobbying the Corporation: Citizen Challenges to Business Authority*, Basic Books, 1978

6 Many of our consumers believe that because these products are manufactured without chlorine, they're safer than traditionally bleached products, and indeed common sense tells us that any reduction in our exposure to toxins, whether its obtained from the products we use or our contact with the general environment, will benefit our health. Unfortunately no research exists to verify these logical assumptions. It's essential that the scientific community increase research into these issues and create more definitive links between toxic exposures and human health. Such verification is crucial to building the case for the purchase of products that are more sustainably produced.

7   When Peter says that "some people are able to masterfully lead complex organizations. We can't explain these successes (other than as blind luck)," I would disagree. Recent research detailed in the book *Talent is Overrated*, which we shall discuss later, clearly indicates that certain types of intentional practice, over 10 or more years, does make a huge difference when it comes to the development of most types of capability.

8   It's both interesting and illustrative to note that if I had decided to quit and sell the business back at the end of 2005, we might have been able to get about $100 million for it. By the beginning of 2009, the company was worth well over $300 million. From the perspective of our shareholders, many of whom are our own employees, the renewed passion that I discovered has been well worth the investment in the developmental process we've made so far.

9   We are working with our supplier to eliminate 1,4-dioxane entirely and expect that the transition will be complete during the first half of 2009.

10 Seventh Generation annually issues what it calls its Corporate Consciousness Report which is prepared according to GRI standards.

11 No good tools have as yet been developed to capture a company's social footprint; this is an area that needs more attention.

12 The use of more efficient washers would also help but only minimally. New generation energy- and water-efficient washing machines can reduce energy use by an average of roughly 38% compared to standard models. Yet even if a consumer owned the most efficient washer available, which would reduce energy use by 50%, their traditional use of high water temperatures would still account for 92.5% of all product-related CO_2 emissions. Only the use of lower temperature washes can dramatically reduce this impact.